STAN AND BRENNA JONES

# FACING THE FACTS

## The Truth About Sex and You

NAVPRESS

A NavPress resource published in alliance
with Tyndale House Publishers, Inc.

# NAVPRESS○.

NavPress is the publishing ministry of The Navigators, an international Christian organization and leader in personal spiritual development. NavPress is committed to helping people grow spiritually and enjoy lives of meaning and hope through personal and group resources that are biblically rooted, culturally relevant, and highly practical.

**For more information, visit www.NavPress.com.**

*To Jennifer*

# CONTENTS

# ACKNOWLEDGMENTS

Each of our children's books benefited greatly from the editorial wisdom of Cathy Davis (for the first versions) and Susan Martins Miller (for the revised versions). Sanna Baker and Carolyn Nystrom provided helpful comments on the first draft of *The Story of Me*, and Lisa, Mark, and Anna McMinn read and gave very helpful feedback on early drafts of *What's the Big Deal?*

We express heartfelt thanks to the many parents who have shared their stories and perspectives, praise and disagreements, about the content of the God's Design for Sex series as we have spoken and taught about this subject around the world. Some of your stories have made it into the revised versions of these books!

Special appreciation goes out to Mark and Lori Yarhouse for their extraordinarily thorough and helpful review of the God's Design for Sex series in preparation for revisions for this new edition, to Elaine Roberts for a remarkably thorough and wise review of all of the children's books, and to Steve Gerali for his careful review of *Facing the Facts*.

Finally, we want to express our deep appreciation and love to our three children, Jennifer, Brandon, and Lindsay. You have, together and individually, enriched our lives far beyond what we could have ever imagined. Thank you for being our living laboratory for working out these ideas, for being so thoughtful and strong, and for loving us all these years.

# THE
# GOD'S DESIGN
## FOR SEX SERIES

Parents, God gave you your sexuality as a precious gift. God gave your children sexuality as well. If handled responsibly, God's gift of sexuality to your child will be a source of blessing and delight.

How can parents help make this happen?

Many forces will push your children to make bad choices about sex. From their earliest years, children are bombarded by destructive, false messages about the nature of sexual intimacy. These messages come through music, television, the Internet, discussions with their friends, school sex-education programs, and so forth. The result? Distressing rates of sexual experimentation, teen pregnancy, abortion, sexually transmitted disease, divorce, and devastated lives.

We believe that God means for Christian parents to be the primary sex educators of their children. First messages are the most powerful; why wait until your child hears the wrong thing and then try to correct the misunderstanding? Sexuality is a beautiful gift; why not present it to children the way God intended? Why not establish yourself as the trusted expert to whom your children can turn to find out God's truth about sexuality?

The GOD'S DESIGN FOR SEX series helps parents shape their children's character, particularly in the area of sexuality. Sex education in the family is less about giving biological information and more about shaping your child's moral character.

How young people handle sexuality in the teen years and beyond is a result of the following five key areas of development. The earlier we start helping children see themselves—including their sexuality—as God does, the stronger they will be as they enter the turbulent teenage years.

- **Needs**: Young people starved for love are more likely to seek having their needs met through sexual experimentation than kids who know they are loved. Strengthening your children's sexual character starts with fostering close parent-child relationships, assisting the development of healthy friendships, and building hope for a meaningful future of personal significance.
- **Values**: Do we teach children to value purity and obedience to God? Or do we let kids learn from the world about immediate pleasure, looking "cool," and fitting in?

- **Beliefs**: Our young people know the core biological facts, but do they also understand how God Himself looks at sex and where sexuality fits into what it means to be a godly man or woman?
- **Skills**: Are we giving our children the abilities to resist peer pressure, stand up for what is right, build meaningful friendships, and form loving relationships as adults?
- **Supports**: Are we helping children grow in the right direction by keeping our relationships with them strong and loving? Are we helping them plug into a vibrant faith community that encourages them to grow and stay close to Jesus?

GOD'S DESIGN FOR SEX is a series of books you can read with your children at ages three to five, five to eight, eight to eleven, and eleven to fourteen. The parents' resource manual, *How and When to Tell Your Kids About Sex: A Lifelong Approach to Shaping Your Child's Sexual Character*, offers a comprehensive understanding of what parents can do to shape their children's sexual character. We don't avoid the hardest subjects, such as sexual abuse or homosexuality. Our goals are to:

- help you understand your role in shaping your children's views, attitudes, and beliefs about sexuality;
- establish God's view of sexuality;
- discuss how to explain and defend the traditional Christian view of sexual morality in these modern times;
- explore how you can most powerfully influence your children to live a life of sexual chastity; and
- equip you to provide your children with the strength necessary to stand by their commitments to traditional Christian morality.

As we've taught and written about the principles for godly, parent-directed sex education in the Christian home, we've heard from parents over and over again, "I think you are right that I should have such conversations, but I don't think I can talk to my children that way.

I wish there were something we could read with our children to get us started in discussing these matters."

The children's books in this series are designed to meet that need. They are meant not to provide all the information kids need but rather to be starting points for Christian parents to discuss sexuality with their children in a manner appropriate to each age. They provide an anchor point for discussions, a jump start to get discussions going. They put the words in your mouths and put the issues out on the table. Don't simply hand these books to your kids to read, because our whole point is to empower you as the parent to shape your children's sexual character. The books are meant to guide the conversations with your children that will deepen your impact on them in the area of sexuality.

Why start early? Because if you as the parent are not teaching your kids about sexuality, they are learning distorted lessons about it from television, the Internet, and playground conversations. If you stand silent on sex while the rest of the world is abuzz about it, kids come to the conclusion that you cannot help them in this key area. If you start now in teaching godly, truthful, tactful, and appropriate lessons about sexuality, your children will trust you more and see you as a mother or father who tells the truth!

## BOOK ONE (AGES THREE TO FIVE): *THE STORY OF ME*

Our most important task with the young child is to lay a spiritual foundation for the child's understanding of sexuality. God loves the human body (and the whole human person) and called it "very good" (Genesis 1:31). Children must see not only their bodies but also their sexual organs as gifts from God.

Young children can begin to develop a wondrous appreciation for God's splendid gift of sexuality by understanding some of the basics of human reproduction, so in this book we discuss the growth of a child inside a mother's body and the birth process. Young children begin to develop a trust for God's Law and to see God as a Lawgiver who has the best interests of His people at heart. God is the giver of good gifts! Finally, we want children to see families as God's intended framework for the nurture and love of children. If you are reading with an adopted child, you'll have an opportunity to talk about how God sometimes creates families that way. We hope you will find *The Story of Me* a wonderful starting point for discussing sexuality with your young child.

## BOOK TWO (AGES FIVE TO EIGHT): *BEFORE I WAS BORN* (BY CAROLYN NYSTROM)

*Before I Was Born* again emphasizes the creational goodness of our bodies, our existence as men and women, and our sexual organs. This book introduces new topics as well, including the growth and change as boys and girls become men and women and a tactful but direct explanation of sexual intercourse between a husband and wife.

If you are reading with an adopted child, use this opportunity to explain that not every couple will have children. If a baby doesn't grow in the mother's womb, the couple might look for a baby or older child to adopt. The birth mother knows that the husband and wife will love their adopted child. This is another way God makes families.

## BOOK THREE (AGES EIGHT TO ELEVEN): *WHAT'S THE BIG DEAL? WHY GOD CARES ABOUT SEX*

This book does three things. First, it reinforces the messages of our first two children's books: the basics of sexual intercourse and the fundamental goodness of our sexuality. Second, it continues the task of deliberately building your child's understanding of why God intends sexual intercourse to be reserved for marriage. Third, it helps you begin the process of "inoculating" your child against the negative moral messages of the world. In *How and When to Tell Your Kids About Sex*, we argue that Christian parents should *not* try to completely shelter their children from the destructive moral messages of the world. Children who grow up in environments where they are never exposed to germs grow up with depleted and ineffectual immune systems for resisting disease. When we shelter them too much, we leave them naive and vulnerable, and we risk communicating that the negative messages of the world are so powerful that Christians cannot even talk about them.

But nor should we just let our kids be inundated with the destructive messages of the world. The principle of inoculation suggests that we should deliberately expose kids to the contrary moral messages they will hear from the world. It should be in *our homes* that our kids first learn that many people in our world do not believe in reserving sex for marriage, and this should also be where they get their first understanding of such problems as teenage pregnancy, AIDS, and homosexuality. But they should be exposed to these realities for a vital purpose: to build their defenses against these terrible problems of our culture.

## Book Four (Ages Eleven to Fourteen): *Facing the Facts: The Truth About Sex and You*

*Facing the Facts: The Truth About Sex and You* builds upon all that has come before in the three previous books but will further prepare your child for puberty. Your child is now old enough for more detailed information about the changes his or her body is about to go through and about the adult body that is soon to be presented as a gift from God. Your child also needs to be reminded about God's view of sexuality, about His loving and beautiful intentions for how this gift should be used. The distorted ways in which our world views sex must be clearly labeled, and our children must be prepared to face views and beliefs contrary to those we are teaching them at home. We attempt to do all this while also talking about the many confusing feelings of puberty and early adolescence. Your child can read this book independently; we encourage you to read it as well and then talk about it together.

All of these books were written as if dialogue were an ongoing reality between mother, father, and children in the home. Yet in some homes, only one parent is willing to talk about sex. Some parents shoulder the responsibility of parenting alone due to separation, divorce, or death. Grandparents may be raising their grandkids. We've tried to be sensitive to adoptive families and families who do not fit the "traditional nuclear family" mold, but we cannot anticipate or respond to all the unique needs of families. Use these books with creativity and thought to meet the needs of your situation.

We have also chosen not to add endnotes with documentation to the children's books. If a specific statement from these books interests you or your child ("Is it really true that almost a million teenagers get pregnant every year?"), you can likely find an endnote directing you to more information in our parents' guidebook, *How and When to Tell Your Kids About Sex.*

We hope these books will be valuable tools in raising a new generation of faithful Christian young people who will have healthy, positive, accepting attitudes about their own sexuality; who will live confident, chaste lives as faithful witnesses to the work of Christ in their lives while they are single; and who will then live fulfilled, loving, rewarding lives as spouses, should they choose to marry.

# INTRODUCTION

In this book we have tried to tell the truth, God's truth, about sex and you. But you are old enough to know that many people disagree about "the truth" when it comes to sex. In the end you, the young person reading this book, will have to make up your mind about what you believe, how you will live, and what you will do. We hope that what we say in this book will help you make decisions in the area of sex that please God, and will make it easier for you to talk with your parents, your youth pastor, and perhaps even your friends about what you believe about this important area of life.

Some people your age are excited about growing up. Others are happy just as they are and dread the changes that lie ahead. The truth is, growing up is both hard and exciting.

You have always had your own unique personality. You have your own sense of humor, beliefs, favorite foods, favorite games, and ways to spend time alone. There is no one else exactly like you.

Being male or female is a very special part of what makes you unique. Up until now you have been either a "man in the making" or a "woman under construction." But after the next few years of real change, no one will think of you as a child anymore. When you are an adult, how you think about your sexuality will have a big impact on who you are. Decisions about what you will and will not do with a boyfriend or girlfriend will have a profound effect on your future. And you are beginning to make up your mind about these things right now! Now is a good time to think through these things and begin to decide what sort of person you will be.

So, we invite you to join us as we try to share with you the truth about sex and you.

# CHAPTER ONE

# WHY IS GOD
# DOING
## THIS TO ME?

Megan can't wait to grow up. As long as she can remember, she has looked forward to being an adult, having the responsibilities and freedoms of an adult, having a grown-up body, and moving on to whatever God has in store for her.

Chris, on the other hand, wishes he wouldn't grow up. He is happy just as he is. He loves his friends; he loves to play. He feels as though everything in his life is just the way it should be, and he sees no good reason why his childhood should end.

How do you feel about growing up? Are you excited or worried? Most of us have a mixture of good and bad feelings about growing up. It's hard! All of us mothers and fathers have experienced the same feelings you are having, though it's hard to remember—and even harder for us to talk about. Some of us asked the question you may be asking: *Why is God doing this to me?* Good question. To answer it, let's start at . . .

## THE BEGINNING

Sex was God's idea. In the beginning, after God made everything else— sun, moon, stars, mountains, sky, plants, birds, fish—God made a man and a woman. Sex was already very much a part of creation before He made people: There are male and female plants, male and female fish, male and female birds and bees and beasts, all made to reproduce themselves through some form of sexual uniting. But sex was and is special for human beings.

At the end of every other day of Creation, God looked out on what He made and saw that it was "good." But on the last day of Creation, when He made man and woman, God saw that it was "very good" (Genesis 1:31). The creation of man and woman was like frosting on the cake of Creation.

> So God created mankind in his own image, in the image of God he created them; male and female he created them.
> God blessed them and said to them, "Be fruitful and increase in number; fill the earth and subdue it. Rule over the fish in the sea and the birds in the sky and over every living creature that moves on the ground." . . .
> God saw all that he had made, and it was very good.
>
> (Genesis 1:27-28,31)

The Bible says that "Adam and his wife were both naked, and they felt no shame" (Genesis 2:25). It's very important to realize what this means. God is happy with the way He designed people as sexual beings. God looked at Adam—his genitals, his ability to become a father, everything that was unique about him as a man—and God was delighted with what He had made. God looked at Eve—her genitals, her ability to carry a baby inside her body, her breasts to nourish that baby, everything else that was unique about her as a woman—and God was very pleased with what He had made.

It was also God's idea that Adam and Eve would be able to have sexual intercourse as a man and wife. In fact, God made their

 **GENITALS** the male or female sexual organs that can be seen between the legs.

bodies so that this would be loving and pleasurable and fun for them. It was God's design that they be able to have children because they had sexual intercourse. That was His plan for populating the earth.

God is happy that He made you a sexual being, with a unique brain, a unique body, unique genitals, and everything else that goes along with your being a young man or a young woman. One of God's main purposes for the changes He has ahead for you is to complete the work of transforming you from a child into an adult.

## Adam Had It Made

You know the story. God made Adam first and put him in the Garden of Eden to take care of it. Adam had the perfect job in the perfect place with a perfect relationship with God. If there was ever anyone who should have been just fine as he was, Adam was that guy. Even so, God wanted things to be even better. He looked at Adam and said, "It is not good for the man to be alone. I will make a helper suitable for him" (Genesis 2:18).

God made each of us with a longing for a special person to share our life with. While we are children, the love of our families can satisfy us. This is what families are meant to do. But God made us in a way that when we become adults, we want something more: We want a special relationship with a special person who is just for us.

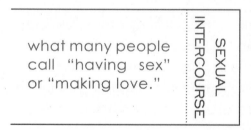

what many people call "having sex" or "making love."

SEXUAL INTERCOURSE

Genesis 2:23 says that after Adam looked around among all the animals and saw there was no partner suitable for him, God made Eve and brought her to him. Adam was so excited about this wonderful gift from God that he cried out,

> This is now bone of my bones
>      and flesh of my flesh;
> she shall be called "woman,"
>      for she was taken out of man.

The writer of Genesis goes on to say, "That is why a man leaves his father and mother and is united to his wife, and they become one flesh" (verse 24).

"One flesh." What a beautiful way to describe the kind of relationship God wants in a marriage blessed by Him. Even though our deepest desire is to know and love God, planted deep in our hearts is a desire for a special love relationship with another human being. God wanted it to be that way.

This is another reason God is changing you, causing your body to grow from a child's body into an adult's body. Adults long to be united with a special person with whom they can have a lifelong love relationship. If you do not have those feelings yet, you probably will within the next few years. You will feel ready to fall in love with someone. The idea of being in love will sound great. And only when your body becomes an adult body can you have the kind of relationship where you will be "glued together" into one flesh with your husband or wife. In fact, having a sexually mature body is a strong and direct part of what makes you ready to have such a love relationship.

## You Could Be a Model

Not everyone gets married. Single people can handle their desire for a special person in a way that honors God and allows them to live vibrant and full lives without having a spouse. But did you know that if God blesses you with marriage, He has a marvelous purpose in mind for your marriage? The Bible teaches that marriages between Christians are meant to be models of the way Christ loves His church.

Several times in the Bible, the joyful time when God welcomes His people home to heaven is described as a wedding feast. It's a joyous celebration when the husband-to-be (Jesus) finally gets to marry the bride He loves (all of us who believe in Jesus). God wanted to put a model right on earth so everyone could see the wonderful love He has for His people. That's one reason He made marriage.

God hopes Christian husbands and wives will form loving, caring, committed relationships. If they do, the people who don't believe in Jesus will be able to look at these marriages and say, "Oh, now I get it. You're saying that the love Jesus has for all of His people is like the love in that Christian marriage, just better and more perfect."

## SUMMING IT UP

So why is God doing this to you? Why does your body have to change into a grown-up body? It's part of God's plan for you. He wants you to become the grown-up, sexual person He meant you to be. He wants to give you a way to meet that deep hunger you will feel for a special relationship with a person who really loves you. He wants you to be a model here on earth of His love for His people, and He wants to make it possible for you to have children should you choose to.

## PUT AWAY YOUR FLASHLIGHT

Many of us have mixed-up feelings about growing up and about our sexuality. Stan was given a small book about sex when he was about your age. He was dying to know more about sex, but he was ashamed and embarrassed for wanting to know—so embarrassed that he read the book only by flashlight at night when he was supposed to be asleep!

> "For this reason a man will leave his father and mother and be united to his wife, and the two will become one flesh." This is a profound mystery—but I am talking about Christ and the church.
>
> (Ephesians 5:31-32)

You don't have to do that with this book. It can be hard for parents and kids to talk together about sex. But even though it's hard, your parents bought you this book because they love you and want you to be able to understand this great gift of sexuality God has given you. They can answer many questions you may have that we won't get to in this book.

Brenna had the kind of relationship with her mother and father that allowed for easy and comfortable discussion about sex. It helped her look forward with confidence toward growing up. If your parents aren't available for this kind of discussion, we hope you can find a trustworthy adult, maybe your youth leader in your church, who can talk frankly with you and answer questions you have.

# CHAPTER TWO

# HOW GOD MADE WOMEN
# AND
# MEN DIFFERENT

**B**oys and girls, women and men, are more alike than different. Young men and women go through many of the same changes as their bodies shift from children's to adults' bodies. Whether you are a boy or a girl, you will go through a growth spurt. You will get taller, heavier, and stronger. You will develop more and darker hair on various parts of your body, especially your arms and legs. You will begin to develop pubic hair (the curly hair that will grow just above your genitals). And many of you will develop what doctors call acne: the pimples, blackheads, and other skin problems caused by the excess oil your body will produce during these changes.

## Okay, So What's Different?

The most obvious difference between men and women is their genitals. Many people use slang words to describe the genitals. We know one family who used the nonsense words "woo-woo" and "ding-ding" for the genitals. Perhaps some of you have used the word "wiener" or "peter" for a man's penis. These kinds of words are not wrong, just silly. Slang can be confusing. We once knew a woman who grew up calling her genitals the "in-between-the-legs"!

Some slang is dirty or rude and should not be used. It takes what God made to be good and treats it as if it were evil. Some of the slang men use to talk about women's bodies is insulting, either because the words are ugly or because they imply that women's bodies are to be "used" by men. This is wrong.

Slang for body parts is often used out of habit, but also because we are uncomfortable talking about our sexuality and feel nervous about using the correct words. In this book we will mostly use the words doctors use, unless those words are too complicated. Because our bodies were made by God and because sex was God's idea, we don't have to use slang.

### WHAT'S UNIQUE ABOUT WOMEN'S BODIES?

Girls and women have three openings between their legs that go up into the inside of their bodies. One is exactly the same as what men have: the anus. This is the opening that your bowel movements come out of. The anus is in the crease between your buttocks in back.

Women have two other openings that go into the interior of their bodies. These openings are hidden in the crease between the labia (which is Latin for "lips") between the woman's legs. When a young girl stands up in the tub to be rinsed off by her mom, all the mother can see of the girl's genitals are the

> Doctors call the outer labia the *labia majora*, which is Latin for "major" or "big" (*majora*) "lips" (*labia*).

two labia and the fold or crease in between them. The **labia** are simply folds of skin that are soft because they are padded with extra muscle and fat as the lips on your face are. Right above the place where the crease between the labia stops is what is called the **mons.** The mons is formed by part of the hipbone underneath the skin. This hipbone sticks out slightly and has lots of muscles attached to it, giving it a soft feel.

The name doctors use for all of a girl's outer genital structures is **vulva,** which means the mons, the labia, and the parts of the genitals between the labia that are not as readily seen. If your doctor ever talks

Outer labia

about the vulva, he or she means this whole genital area. Some women just call this their genitals or "privates."

The structures between the labia usually cannot be seen except by deliberately spreading the legs and looking at them. Because the genitals of boys are on the outside and stick out a bit, and because boys actually handle their genitals when they wash themselves or go to the bathroom, boys are more familiar with the way their genitals look than are girls. There is nothing wrong with a girl looking at the remarkable way God made her. But to do so, she has to bend down and look or use a hand mirror.

*Mons* is Latin for "mound."

God placed four structures between the outer labia. One is easy to see on some women and not so easy to see on others. This is the inner labia or lips, folds or looseness of the skin, which goes in from the outer labia

2 5

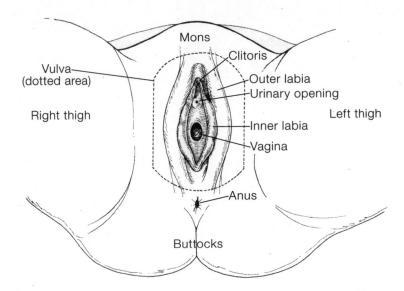

Mons
Clitoris
Vulva
(dotted area)
Outer labia
Urinary opening
Right thigh
Left thigh
Inner labia
Vagina
Anus
Buttocks

toward the vagina. The inner labia or lips have many nerve endings that make them very sensitive to touch. They seem to be one more gift from God to help a woman find pleasure in making love to her husband.

The woman's vagina is the easiest to see. The **vagina** is an interior tube that goes inside the body for three or four inches. It is made up of muscles covered with tissue like the tissue on the inside of your mouth. The opening of the vagina looks like a small hole that opens into the inside of the woman's body. This opening is smaller in many girls who have not yet had sex because God made a piece of skin called the hymen to partially cover it. The hymen helps protect the inside of the vagina when a girl is young. When a woman has sex, this piece of skin is broken or stretched.

> Doctors call the inner labia the *labia minora*, which is Latin for "minor" or "little" (*minora*) "lips" (*labia*).

In some parts of the world, the hymen is considered proof that the woman has never had sex before, but this is not a valid test. Some girls are born with thick hymens, and some are born with hardly any. Also, hymens on many girls naturally stretch or break from sports like track or gymnastics.

The vagina was made by God to do two things. One is to be the "birth canal" through which a baby comes out of the woman's womb and into the world. Most of the time, the vagina is relaxed and somewhat closed, so it is hard to believe that this muscular tube can expand to let a baby's head and body pass through.

> The hymen is a circle of skin that makes the opening of the vagina smaller and helps protect a girl's vagina as she grows up.

The other main purpose of the vagina is to take in the husband's penis during sexual intercourse. The vagina has a number of nerve endings that help it feel good when it is touched or rubbed. This is what happens when the husband's penis moves back and forth in the wife's vagina during sexual intercourse.

When a husband and wife have sexual intercourse, they move their bodies back and forth so that the husband's penis moves back and forth in the woman's vagina. This would not feel good if the skin of his penis and her vagina were dry like the skin on your arm. For that reason, God made the woman's vagina so that when she feels full of love for her husband and is excited about being close to him and making

> During childbirth, a woman's vagina can stretch to the size of a baby's head, which is about the size of a small cantaloupe!

love to him (this is what is called being sexually aroused), her vagina makes a watery, slippery **lubrication** that makes it very comfortable for her to have sexual intercourse.

This lubrication doesn't happen only when you are married, however. After a young woman has developed an adult body, she will sometimes feel her vagina get slightly wet. This can happen when she thinks about a boyfriend she is really attracted to and begins to feel some sexual arousal or sometimes after she has dreams at night. This is perfectly normal and not something to be ashamed of or feel guilty about. Remember, there is nothing wrong about feeling sexual excitement like this; you are simply responding as a sexual person the way God made you.

The third structure that can be seen between the labia, though with some difficulty, is the opening through which your urine comes out. This opening is called the **urinary opening** and is located just above the vagina (toward the mons). Some girls think their urine comes out through their vagina, but it doesn't. Urine comes from your bladder through a tube called the **urethra** and then out of this tiny urinary opening.

The final structure that is between a woman's labia is her **clitoris**. The clitoris is a small bump that is above the vagina and the urethra and below where the two labia come together. It is very sensitive to the touch. In fact, of all the parts of the woman's genitals, the clitoris has more nerve endings and is more wonderfully sensitive to touch than any other. It appears that God made the clitoris for only one purpose: to give a woman pleasure from being touched there by her husband and having sexual intercourse with him.

Women and men basically respond the same way to the pleasure of sex. Most married people say sex with their spouse brings them great joy. (Those who don't feel that way usually say it is because they don't love each other very much, because they can't talk about sex and don't understand each other, because they feel that sex is bad, or because something is wrong with one or both persons' bodies.) Husbands and wives both say touching each other all over, but especially on the genitals, feels wonderful. So does having sexual intercourse. If this pleasure continues, it can get stronger and stronger. If the couple keeps giving each other pleasure, both the husband and the wife can have an **orgasm**. An orgasm is when the pleasure of their bodies suddenly gets very strong and their bodies tremble a little all over. After an orgasm, a married couple usually feels very close to each other, with a sense of satisfaction and calm. Part of the joy of marriage is learning what gives your spouse pleasure and then being able to show your love to your spouse in that way.

## WHAT ABOUT BREASTS?

Breasts of both girls and boys look alike. Both boys and girls have nipples that are darker than the skin around them and breasts that are flat against the chest. But in adolescence, young men's breasts don't enlarge, while young women's do. No matter what the size, women's breasts are made of the same parts. On the outside, a woman's breast is made of the same skin as the area around the breast with a nipple of darker skin at the center. The ribs and muscles of a woman's chest are the same as those of a man. The difference is what lies between the muscle of the woman's chest and the skin. The inside of her breast is formed of two parts: milk glands that connect to the woman's nipples through tiny tubes, and fatty tissue that makes her breasts soft. Women with small breasts have the same number of milk glands as women with large breasts. The only thing that makes one woman's breasts larger than another's is the amount of fatty tissue in the breast. The milk glands in a pregnant woman's breasts do not usually produce any milk until after she delivers a baby. There is no milk in the breasts of women who have never been pregnant. Breasts vary from woman to woman, just as their faces and hands do.

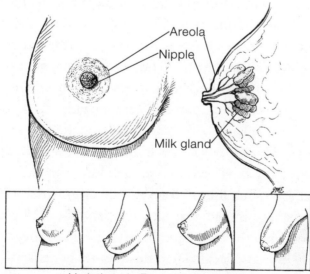

Areola

Nipple

Milk gland

Variations in Breast Appearance

Women's bodies are a complex miracle! God made women in His image and blessed them with sexuality so they can enjoy a beautiful and exciting sexual relationship with their husbands and also experience the joy of pregnancy, childbirth, and nursing a child. What a great idea God had!

## So What's Unique About Men's Bodies?

Men have two openings into the inside of their bodies that are located between their legs. Just like women, men have an anus for bowel movements located in the crease between the buttocks.

While a woman's vagina and clitoris are hidden from sight most of the time, a man's genitals are easy to see. Most obvious is the man's **penis**. The penis is a soft, springy tube of tissue and has three main parts. The first is the shaft, which is the main part of the penis from where it comes out of the body to near the head, or end. The skin on the shaft of the penis is a bit rough, sort of like skin on the man's arm or leg, except it doesn't usually have much hair on it.

The second part of the penis is the foreskin. The foreskin is like a continuation of loose skin from the shaft of the penis that covers over the head of the penis with an opening at the end.

Some baby boys have most of their foreskin cut off while they are still in the hospital after being born. This is called **circumcision**. After the circumcision, the head of the penis, instead of being hidden by the foreskin, is now exposed all the time. The best estimates are that somewhere between half to two-thirds of baby boys born in America are circumcised. Customs differ within and between cultures though. For instance, babies born in Latin American families in the U.S. are usually not circumcised, and most boys born in Europe are not circumcised. Nearly all Jewish baby boys are circumcised, however; this has been the practice of all Jews since the time of Abraham (see Genesis 17:10-14). Some early Christians argued that all Christians should be circumcised, just like Jews, but the early church, just a few years after the death and resurrection of Jesus, decided that this was not necessary (see Acts 15:5-21). So some Christians are circumcised and some aren't! Doctors

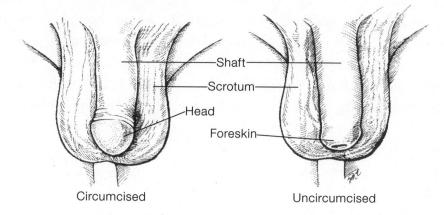

Circumcised          Uncircumcised

disagree as to which is healthier, but men who have been circumcised find it a little easier to keep the penis clean. Men who haven't been circumcised should pay careful attention to cleanliness by pulling back the foreskin when they bathe and washing around the head of the penis.

The third part of the man's penis is the head, or **glans**. The skin on the glans is different from the skin on the shaft; it is very smooth and sensitive. There is a hole, or opening, at the end of the man's penis through which he passes urine. This is the second opening to the inside of his body.

Underneath the penis is a "bag" called the **scrotum**. Right under the skin of this bag is a layer of muscle. Inside the scrotum are the two **testes**. You can't see the testes from outside the body, but a boy can feel the testes when he touches his scrotum. They feel like two balls inside the sack, and that is why it is very common in slang terms to call a man's testes his "balls."

One of the jobs of the scrotum is to move and change automatically so the temperature of the testes inside it is just right. When a boy is very warm, the scrotum is loose and hangs down more so the testes inside can be cooler because they are farther away from his warm body. But when a boy is cold, the scrotum tightens up, pulling the testes inside up tight against the boy's warm body.

The testes have two important jobs. First, they produce the hormone testosterone, which is a special chemical that changes a boy's body into a man's body and keeps him looking like a man throughout his life. Without his testes, a man would not develop a beard or be capable of developing a greater mass of muscles than the typical woman. The other important thing that the testes do is produce sperm, which are essential for having children. The testes move closer and further away from the man's body to maintain the right temperature for the continuing production of sperm.

> The hormone that makes a boy into a man is called testosterone.

Men's bodies are also a complex miracle! Men are made in God's image, and their sexuality is a gift from God. Their bodies are made so they can enjoy sex every bit as much as their wives do. And their bodies were made so they can become fathers. Let's hear it for God's great ideas!

# CHAPTER THREE

# THE CHANGES
# AHEAD
## FOR GIRLS

Sometime between ages nine and fifteen, most often around age eleven, a girl's body begins to become a woman's body. There is no right time for these changes to begin. Some girls' bodies start to change early, others late. Everyone is different. Girls who start going through these changes early often feel odd and may get teased by other kids for beginning to develop breasts or for growing so fast. Girls who go through the changes late also might feel odd and get teased, especially for looking like a young girl when their classmates look more mature.

God has different timing for different people. There is nothing you can do to change your body's timing. If you are troubled because your body is changing earlier or later than your friends' bodies, please try not to worry about this or feel that there is something wrong with you.

## THE INSIDE STORY

We already talked about the sexual organs you can see from the outside: a girl's breasts, labia, vagina, clitoris, and so forth. Now let's talk about what is on the inside.

Remember that a woman's vagina goes up into her body for three or four inches. The vagina has an opening inside of it called the **cervix** that goes farther up inside the body. The cervix is like a tiny donut with the hole in the middle squeezed closed. That hole in the center

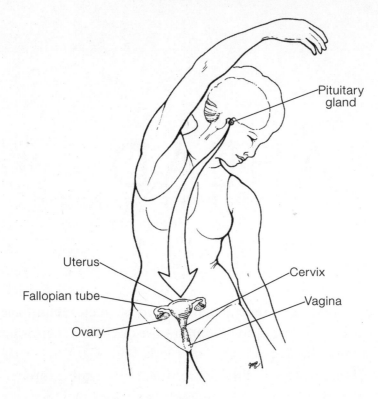

Pituitary
gland

Uterus

Cervix

Fallopian tube

Vagina

Ovary

of the cervix opens into the inside of the woman's **uterus**, or womb. The cervix is the very bottom part of the woman's uterus. The uterus is a muscular organ that provides a secure place for a baby to grow for nine months and also delivers the life-giving air, food, and water the baby needs. The uterus is powerful enough to squeeze the baby out of the woman's body when it's time to be born—the way we squeeze toothpaste out of a toothpaste tube.

To find out how big your uterus is, squeeze your fist closed and look at it. A woman's uterus is generally about the size of her closed fist. But when a woman is nine months pregnant and about to give birth, her uterus has expanded to almost the size of a small grocery bag, big enough to hold a baby!

At the top the uterus branches out into the **fallopian tubes**, which go out from the uterus to the **ovaries**, one to the right and one to the left. The ovaries are very much like the man's testes and do two main things: produce eggs and produce the hormones that make a girl into a woman, specifically estrogen and progesterone. The two ovaries are small and round, located up inside a woman's body on each side of a spot just below her belly button.

## PUBER . . . WHAT?

Puberty is an awkward and funny word that means the time when a person's body is maturing sexually. This time usually lasts one to two years. How does the body know when to start puberty? No one is quite sure, but it is the "master gland" of the brain, the **pituitary gland**, that signals the girl's body to begin puberty. It sends chemical signals to other parts of the brain and to the ovaries to release their special chemicals, called hormones, which cause her body to begin changing.

> The hormones that make a girl into a woman are estrogen and progesterone.

## WHAT HAPPENS FIRST?

The first change of puberty that most girls notice is that their breasts begin to develop. A young girl's nipple feels pretty much the same as the skin around the nipple. When breast growth begins, however, it starts right underneath her nipple so that she begins to feel a little lump. Doctors call this lump a breast bud. For some girls the lump is very soft, and for others it is hard. A few girls experience a little discomfort or sensitivity in their breast buds, but this usually does not last long. Slowly, over a period of two to four years, the breasts begin to grow to their adult size through the growth of fatty tissue under the nipples and around the milk ducts. As in the rest of the body, this growth can come in spurts.

> PUBERTY
> the time during which a child's body is changed into an adult's body.

Breast development occurs at different rates for different girls, and even at different rates in the same girl. For instance, many girls will notice one breast taking a couple of months to catch up with the development of the other. This can make finding a bra that fits well quite a challenge!

There is no such thing as a "normal" breast size. Alyssa wishes her breasts were larger, while Laticia wishes hers were smaller. Breast size varies as much as people size: Some tiny people measure barely over four feet tall, while giant people, such as professional basketball players, tower over seven feet tall.

## IS BIGGER REALLY BETTER?

What does breast size mean? Does it make a difference? Breast size has absolutely nothing to do with a woman's ability to give milk to a baby through nursing. All women's breasts, no matter how small or large, have the same number of milk glands and the same capacity to give milk when they nurse a baby. Women who have smaller breasts usually notice that their breasts are a bit bigger when they are nursing a baby, but then their breasts go back to their previous size when they stop. Women's breasts differ in size because of the amount of fatty tissue in them. Women with bigger breasts simply have more fatty tissue in them.

Because a woman's breasts have sensitive nerve endings, most women find it very pleasurable when their husbands touch their breasts. This is a normal part of making love and expressing affection in marriage. The size of a woman's breasts makes little difference in how much pleasure she gets from having her breasts touched. In fact, women who have very large breasts sometimes have less feeling in their breasts than women with average or smaller breasts.

Sadly, some men think big breasts are important for a woman to be attractive and will pay more attention to women with large breasts. Preferring women with one size of breasts over another is sort of like preferring women with blue eyes to women with brown eyes. Both are beautiful. Because women can't do anything (besides have surgery) to increase or decrease the size of their breasts (don't believe those ads for exercises, creams, or pills; they don't work!), we urge you not to worry about breast size. Any young man who is using breast size as his main guide for whether you are attractive or not is not worth your time and energy! It is becoming a more common practice for women to have breast enlargement surgery, but this seems a risky and extreme reaction to having breasts that are average size or smaller.

About the time breast development starts, a girl's pubic hair begins to grow and her labia darken slightly in color. At first, pubic hair tends to be straight and fine. After several months, however, the hair gradually becomes more curly and thicker. Women differ in terms of how thick their hair is in the genital area. Some have a very light growth of hair, while others have a lot of hair and may choose to remove some of it before wearing a swimsuit in public.

## BUT THAT'S NOT ALL

While her breasts are beginning to develop, a girl's internal organs and genitals are beginning to change as well. The biggest changes happen so that when the right time comes, she will be able to get pregnant and carry a baby. And that's why the **menstrual period** is so important.

A young woman usually has her first menstrual period about twelve to eighteen months after her breasts begin to develop. Let's first talk about what a period is and then about how to handle it.

A woman goes through a rhythmic cycle about every twenty-eight days. Some women's cycles are longer (around thirty-five days) while others are shorter (around twenty-three days). Often the first few cycles of young women just beginning to menstruate are irregular and unpredictable, but they begin to become more regular later.

For most women, the couple of days before menstruation begins are a time of mild discomfort. During this premenstrual time, a woman might notice some mild cramps in her stomach or be a little more tired than usual and perhaps headachy. She might be more down or grumpy than usual. Every woman is different, and most women don't experience this time before their period as any big deal. Part of what will determine how you feel is your attitude toward your body. Women who feel good about being a woman and have a positive attitude seem to have fewer problems with this time before their period.

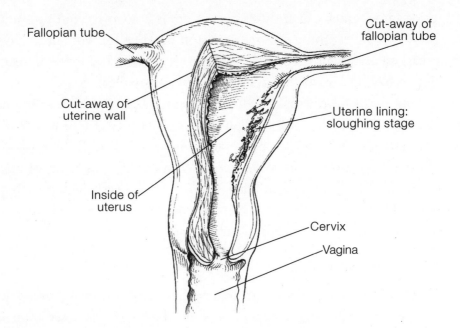

Fallopian tube

Cut-away of
fallopian tube

Cut-away of
uterine wall

Uterine lining:
sloughing stage

Inside of
uterus

Cervix

Vagina

When menstruation begins, a small amount of blood passes from the uterus through the cervix and vagina. The blood flow is typically heavier on the first and second days of the menstrual period and then begins to slow down. Some women will have the blood flow for only three days, while others will have it for up to six days. A woman's period can change from time to time depending on how healthy she is, how much stress she is under, and other factors.

## WHY HAVE A MENSTRUAL PERIOD, ANYWAY?

The answer is tied to a woman's ability to get pregnant. Even when a woman is single and not having sexual intercourse, her body is still getting ready each month to carry a baby—to be pregnant. To understand a woman's menstrual cycle, let's start with the day she begins her menstrual bleeding.

The average woman menstruates for three to six days in each cycle. During the next ten to twelve days after the woman's menstrual bleeding stops, her body is preparing an egg to be released by one of her ovaries. The release of the egg (called ovulation) usually happens

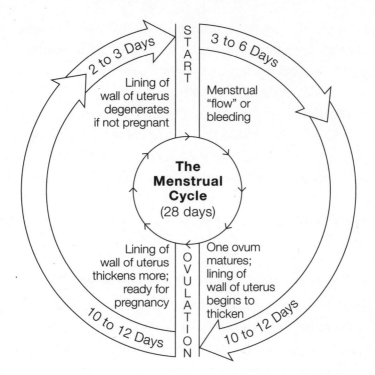

The Menstrual Cycle (28 days)

START

2 to 3 Days — Lining of wall of uterus degenerates if not pregnant

3 to 6 Days — Menstrual "flow" or bleeding

10 to 12 Days — Lining of wall of uterus thickens more; ready for pregnancy

OVULATION

10 to 12 Days — One ovum matures; lining of wall of uterus begins to thicken

around fourteen or fifteen days after her period started, but it can be as soon as ten days or as late as eighteen days after.

As the time for her ovary to release the egg nears, the woman's body begins to prepare the inside of her uterus to nourish a baby in case that egg gets fertilized and a child is conceived. That unborn baby will be nourished from the blood stored inside the wall of the mother's uterus, so every month the wall of the uterus has to be made ready to nourish a baby. It does this by building up a lining that is very rich in blood and tissue, perfect for keeping the tiny baby alive. Building up the lining of the uterus begins several days before the egg is released, and after ovulation the woman's body finishes getting her uterus completely ready for a possible pregnancy and keeps the uterus ready for the next ten to twelve days after ovulation.

If the woman has sex and her egg joins with a sperm, she conceives a baby. When the baby is a round ball of cells only a few days old, it will attach to the uterus and draw its nourishment from that uterine wall throughout the pregnancy. However, if the woman does not become pregnant, the rich lining of blood and blood vessels, which her body built up just days before, begins to dissolve over a period of a few days. After those few days, menstruation begins again.

Menstruation is the result of the uterus shedding the extra tissue, blood vessels, and blood that it had stored up in anticipation of pregnancy. So the flow that comes out of a woman's vagina is actually blood mixed with cells of tissue from the lining of the uterus, including the unfertilized egg. In this way, her uterus "cleans out" the unused preparation for pregnancy and clears the way for new preparations in the next cycle.

## What If I'm at School When My Period Starts?

It can be a little nerve-racking to know that your first period could come at any time! Even though you know that the first period usually occurs twelve to eighteen months after your breasts begin to develop, that's still quite a wide window of time.

Most girls don't feel confident that they will know what to do when their period starts. *What if I'm in school? At a party? At the mall? At a sleepover? Alone at home?* Most girls find out that they have started their periods when, after a couple days of not feeling quite right, they go to the bathroom and find some light red blood on their panties or on the tissue when they wipe themselves.

Your parents can buy you some sanitary pads that can be stored in the bathroom and carried in your purse for when your period begins. These are thin pads of cottony paper that soak up the menstrual flow and keep you clean. When you get your first period, all you have to do is to change your panties and begin wearing a pad, which sticks to your panties between the legs. Most women's flow is heaviest during the first two days. During this time, they change pads several times a day. Later in the period, when there is much less blood flow, they might change less often.

Another way to take care of the menstrual flow is to use a tampon. A tampon is made of the same kind of absorbent material as the pad, except it is packed tighter and is in the shape of a small tube. A woman pushes the tampon gently into her vagina with either her finger or an applicator that comes with the tampons. The tampon then absorbs the bleeding inside of her vagina instead of letting it flow out. Inserting a tampon can be a little uncomfortable the first few times a young woman does it, but it does not hurt and quickly becomes as normal as wiping yourself after going to the bathroom.

The tampon comes with a string attached that hangs out of the young woman's vagina just slightly. Pulling on the string removes the tampon so it can be thrown away. It's important to change tampons regularly. Some women who do not change them often enough develop health problems. Women should change their tampons every three to four hours during the day. They can leave them in while they sleep, but they should put a fresh one in before they go to sleep and then change it when they wake up.

Many girls are not comfortable using a tampon when they first begin having periods because they feel funny about pushing something into their vaginas, especially when they've never had sexual intercourse. Using a tampon, however, has nothing to do with sexual intercourse and so this should not worry you. Girls sometimes decide to use tampons because they want to do an activity like gymnastics or swimming that they can't do while wearing a pad. Whether you use pads or tampons is a personal choice that you can probably talk over with your mother or another trusted woman.

If you think ahead about what you will do when you get your first period, you will have no need to fear. If it occurs at school, you can go to the school nurse or your teacher for help. If you have a male teacher, you can simply say, "I would like to see the nurse because I don't feel well." A school nurse will have a supply of pads on hand to help. If your first period comes when you are at a public place, like a restaurant or mall, you will find that most public bathrooms have a sanitary-napkin dispenser. If nothing else, you can fold a bit of toilet tissue into the crotch of your panties until you can get a pad.

Many girls find it helpful to keep track of their periods on a calendar to get a better sense of what their regular cycle is going to be. As we said earlier, some women's cycles are shorter and some are longer. When your cycle becomes regular, you can predict fairly accurately when you might begin your period. This can help you plan when to carry pads or tampons with you. Some young women become regular very quickly, within a few months, but many have irregular and unpredictable menstrual periods into their late teenage years. Do not worry if your periods are irregular for several years after you start menstruating.

## A Blessing or a Curse?

There is no one point when you stop being a child and become a woman. Some people with very mature bodies are as childish as any eight-year-old. And some fourteen-year-olds who have not gone through puberty yet can be quite mature. But having your first period is a clear signal that your body is becoming an adult body. This is the reason some mothers celebrate the first period of their daughters. Women menstruate because of God's splendid design for getting their bodies ready for pregnancy each month. Menstruation is a sign that you could get pregnant if you had sexual intercourse. You have made another big step toward adulthood, and that's something to be happy about!

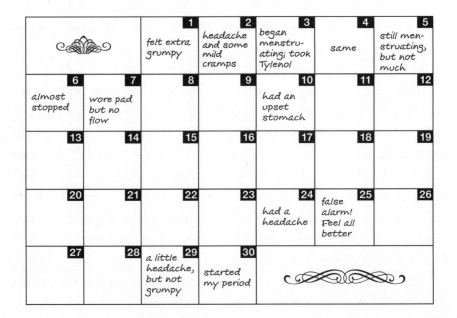

| | | **1** felt extra grumpy | **2** headache and some mild cramps | **3** began menstru-ating; took Tylenol | **4** same | **5** still men-struating, but not much |
|---|---|---|---|---|---|---|
| **6** almost stopped | **7** wore pad but no flow | **8** | **9** | **10** had an upset stomach | **11** | **12** |
| **13** | **14** | **15** | **16** | **17** | **18** | **19** |
| **20** | **21** | **22** | **23** had a headache | **24** | **25** false alarm! Feel all better | **26** |
| **27** | **28** | **29** a little headache, but not grumpy | **30** started my period | | | |

But not all women feel good about having their periods. Have you ever heard a woman describe her period as "the curse"? She may be among those few who have tough physical symptoms with their period, like bad headaches or strong cramps. Even if your mother or older sister has these kinds of symptoms, that doesn't mean the same thing will happen to you. But if it does, you can talk to your mother and your doctor about how to relieve the symptoms of your period.

Some people feel bad about their period because bleeding just seems dirty. Others feel that because the opening of the vagina is just a few inches from the anus and right next to the urinary opening, the menstrual flow must be dirty in the same way as bowel movements and urine. But the vagina is very clean. God made the vagina to clean itself just as He made your eyes to clean themselves with tears. You have never washed out your eyes with soap, but you don't worry about them being dirty. Nor is the menstrual flow "diseased" or "bad blood." It's no dirtier than the blood coming from a cut on your arm.

One reason that some women think of their period as dirty is that in the Old Testament the Jews were told by God (in the Law of Moses) that women who were having their period were unclean (see Leviticus 15:19-24). Does this mean God is disgusted by menstruation or that men should be disgusted with women who are menstruating? Absolutely not! Why, then, is this in the Bible? To understand this, you must first know that in the Bible, the word unclean does not mean "dirty" the way we use that word today: full of germs and unhealthy to touch. And things that were unclean were not necessarily sinful. And since the time of the book of Acts (chapters 10 and 11), Christians haven't regarded the things the Old Testament calls "unclean" to be any problem for us. We aren't made special or different by our rules; we are different because we follow Jesus!

So celebrate your body! Your body is a miracle—every part of it. You were designed and crafted exactly as God intended. You have a vagina, uterus, ovaries, breasts, and everything else that is special about women because God wanted it that way. He looked on Eve and declared her "very good!" He feels the same way about you.

# CHAPTER FOUR

# THE CHANGES
# AHEAD
## FOR BOYS

If you are an eleven- or twelve-year-old boy, there is a good chance your body has not yet begun the changes we call puberty: the time when a child's body is changing into an adult body. Most boys go through puberty between the ages of twelve and fourteen, while girls go through it between ages ten and thirteen. Boys get a later start in maturing than girls do.

At the end of puberty you won't be fully grown, but *sexually* your body will function like a man's body. If a thirteen-year-old boy has gone through puberty, he could become a father if he had sexual intercourse with a woman.

### Take Your Time

Just like girls, boys go through puberty at their own time. Some boys begin the process at age eleven or even younger, while others don't go through puberty until they're sixteen or seventeen. You might ask your dad when he went through puberty, because you will probably go through it around the same age he did.

The age you go through puberty has no effect on how healthy you are or whether you will have a satisfying marriage. However, boys who go through puberty late are sometimes teased by other boys at school. If you know boys who are going through puberty late, you can help protect and support them as they go through this process. Being called names can hurt and discourage a boy.

## SIGNS OF THE TIMES

The first outward sign that a boy is beginning the process of puberty is usually the growth of pubic hair just above the penis. This hair often starts out fine and straight but within six months or so usually becomes darker, thicker, and curlier. Most men also have some thin hair growing on their scrotum.

Soon after a boy begins to grow pubic hair, he will probably have a general growth spurt. During the puberty period, the penis and scrotum have a growth spurt of their own, growing a bit faster than the rest of the body and changing some in appearance. The skin on a boy's penis and scrotum looks a lot like the skin on the rest of his body, but as he becomes a man, this skin gets a bit darker and rougher than the rest of his skin.

As his penis and scrotum begin to grow, a young man often worries whether these parts are the "normal" size and look all right. Remember that the size of your penis changes a lot depending on how you are feeling, what the temperature is, and so forth. If you're cold, your scrotum tucks up against your body and your penis shrinks down to its smaller size. If you're warm and comfortable, the scrotum hangs loose and the penis is longer.

## WISE ABOUT SIZE

However, there *are* differences in penis sizes. When young men shower together in school, they often glance around to see how they compare with other boys. It's obvious that different young men have different penis sizes, depending upon whether they have gone through puberty or not. But it's true that some men just have larger penises than others.

You probably already know that an **erection** is when a young man's penis gets hard and sticks out from his body instead of hanging loosely as it normally does. When men have erections, most of the differences in penis size disappear; the differences that remain aren't that great.

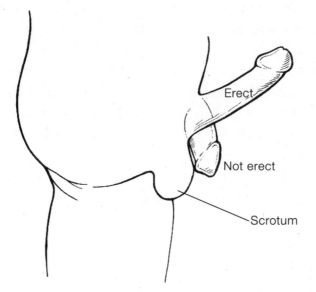

In spite of what some boys whisper in jokes and locker-room bragging, the size of a man's penis doesn't seem to matter at all and has nothing to do with how much of a man he is or how strong or brave he is. It especially has nothing to do with how much fun and pleasure he will have with his wife sexually when he is married. So the size of your penis is nothing to worry about.

## How Do I Look?

Another concern that young men have is the way their scrotum looks. It's normal for one of the testes inside the scrotum to hang a little lower and a little more in front than the other.

During puberty, boys begin to get facial hair, starting with a few whiskers at the corners of the mouth (the beginnings of a mustache) or on the tip of the chin. Sideburns usually begin to thicken and grow down farther than they used to. A man's beard comes in gradually. Some men are able to grow a full beard as early as age fifteen, and others are unable to grow a thick beard even when they are forty. Men also begin to get more hair in their armpits, on their arms and legs, and on their chests. There are big differences in how much hair men get in their beards, underarms, and chests, but this has nothing to do with how much of a man they are or whether they will be a good husband.

A young man's growth continues for some time after puberty. There are big differences in when men reach their full size. Some are at their full size by the time they are fifteen, but others continue growing into their early twenties. Before puberty, a boy can exercise all he wants and still not develop big muscles. After puberty, young men who exercise regularly can become stronger and their muscles will get bigger. Some men's bodies are built in such a way that exercise produces much bigger muscles than those of other men who exercise just as much. This is just a difference between individuals.

## THE INSIDE STORY

We've been talking about the changes that are easy to see. But all this time changes have been happening on the inside as well.

It is the master gland at the bottom of the brain, the **pituitary**, that triggers the boy's body to begin the transformation into a man's body. The pituitary causes the boy's testes to begin making **testosterone**, the chemical that causes all of the major changes in his body. It is the testosterone circulating through the blood that causes all of the outside changes: the growth of body hair, the growth of muscles, and greater height and weight. But testosterone also causes changes on the inside.

Your testes feel like hard balls but are actually a densely packed group of tubes. On the inside of these tubes, sperm will be produced, while in the space between the tubes, the sexual hormone testosterone is produced. Testosterone is carried away from the testes by the blood vessels that nourish the testes. The many tubes inside each testicle (the singular form of testes) empty into a tiny tube called the vas deferens that goes from inside your scrotal sack up inside your body. These two tubes, one from each testicle, go inside your body and around your bladder (the muscle bag that holds your urine) and join together inside the prostate.

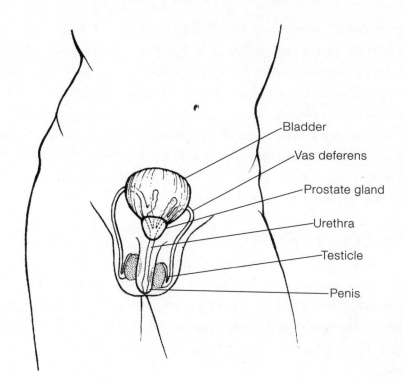

The **urethra** is the tube that goes from the bladder out to the tip of your penis. Under the bladder, wrapped around the urethra, is a gland called the prostate. It is inside the prostate that the two vas deferens tubes from the testes connect into the urethra. So the urethra that opens at the end of a man's penis has three organs that empty into it—the bladder and two testes. The prostate is the place where these three all connect to the urethra.

> The tubes in a man's testes are so tiny that if you were to uncoil the tubes in one testicle, they would stretch more than a quarter mile. That's tiny!

## THE SPERM GAME

At the same time that your testes start producing testosterone, they begin producing sperm. The average man produces a hundred million sperm every twenty-four hours! Just to get an idea of that, imagine seventy thousand people sitting in a football stadium for a game. To produce a hundred million sperm in a day, a young man's testes must produce about as many sperm every minute as there are people in that football stadium!

Testosterone also starts the prostate and other small, previously inactive glands working. They begin to produce a fluid that is stored up by the young man's body and mixes with the sperm coming out of his body when he has an ejaculation.

## What's All the Excitement About?

One of the biggest changes of puberty is that a young man begins to experience more sexual excitement or arousal, which usually causes more erections. Most boys have experienced an erection (or in slang terms, "hard-on") at different times in their life; even baby boys get erections. But men certainly get more erections after they go through puberty.

The skin of the penis has lots of nerves in it, especially on the head, or glans. These nerves are made by God in such a way that it feels good for the penis to be touched or rubbed. In this way, the head of the penis is just like a woman's clitoris; it was designed by God for pleasure! One of the changes of puberty is that the pleasure a young man feels from his penis being touched increases. It feels much better than it ever did before. And when he feels pleasure from his penis being touched, he may get an erection.

After a boy goes through puberty, he naturally becomes more interested in girls and thinks more frequently about sex. When he thought about sex before, he didn't have any particular reaction. But when a young man thinks about sex, he often feels sexually aroused or excited, and he may begin to notice his penis having an erection.

Men often have erections three or four times every night, during the periods of deepest sleep when we are also most likely to dream. In fact, it is common for men to wake up in the morning with an erection. Having erections at these times doesn't appear to have anything to do with whether they were dreaming at all or whether a dream was about sex in any way. Rather, there is something about the way the body relaxes deeply in these periods of sleep that is connected to having more blood flow to the penis.

Sometimes young men get erections for no obvious reason. They don't remember thinking about sex or anything in particular, and their penis hasn't been touched, but they suddenly find themselves getting an erection. This can happen, for example, when they are cooling down after exercising hard or playing a demanding sport. This is just a normal part of growing up. It's very important for boys to realize that even if this happens at awkward times, like when they are sitting in class or watching a movie, people generally can't tell that they have an erection, and it's simply nothing to worry about.

### How Does an Erection Occur?

The penis has skin on the outside. The urethra, the tube that passes urine, runs down the center. The rest of the penis inside the skin and around the urethra is made up of a spongy, soft tissue that is different from any other tissue in the man's body. When a man feels pleasure from his penis being touched or rubbed, God made his body to respond to that pleasure by automatically sending more blood to the penis. This blood gets packed into the spongy tissue of the penis so tightly that it makes the penis harder and bigger. It is sort of like filling up a water balloon. A balloon with no water in it is completely limp, but a balloon that has filled with water gets harder, heavier, and stiffer. That is exactly what happens to a man's penis as it fills with blood. When it is not erect, a man's penis will usually be three or four inches long. When he gets an erection, his penis may be about twice that size, and it goes from dangling downward loosely to pointing outward from his body and being stiff.

Sometime during puberty a young man becomes able to have an **ejaculation**. From that time on, he is capable of becoming a father. He is certainly not ready to become a father or to have sex, but he is now producing sperm that can get a young woman pregnant.

When does an ejaculation occur? If a man gets more and more sexually excited, his excitement eventually builds to a peak. This happens when a couple is having sexual intercourse. The man begins to have an erection when he is kissing and hugging his wife. If they then have sexual intercourse, the man finds this to be very exciting, and the pleasure builds up until he feels a burst of intense pleasure. This burst of intense pleasure is called an **orgasm**. At the same time as the orgasm, a mixture of sperm and other fluids spurt out of his penis. That is an ejaculation.

How does this happen? When a young man's testes begin to produce sperm, the sperm are stored in the tube just outside of the testes. If the sperm are not ejaculated out of his body in a few days, they die and are reabsorbed by the body. They are replaced by freshly made sperm. Moments before the orgasm, the man's sperm move quickly from the testes through the vas deferens tubes to the prostate. These tiny tubes are actually made of muscles that squeeze and release quickly all along their length, in just the same way that you squeeze toothpaste out of a tube.

> **SEMEN** The milky white fluid that is a mixture of sperm and fluids from the prostate and other glands. Semen is spurted out of the penis when a man has an ejaculation.

In the prostate the sperm mix with fluid from the prostate and other glands to make the milky white fluid, called semen, that will be ejected out of the penis. The other fluids that make up the semen are specially designed to assist the sperm to live inside a woman's body and to reach the egg to make a baby. The semen enters the urethra, which uses the same kind of muscular squeezing and releasing to push (ejaculate) the semen from the prostate out through the end of the penis.

The amount of fluid that comes out of the urethra during an ejaculation is only a small amount, about a teaspoon or a little more. Inside that teaspoon of semen are 150 to 600 million sperm so tiny that if you were to remove them from the other fluids that make up the semen, there would be no noticeable decrease in the amount of fluid. Sperm can be seen only with a microscope; they are incredibly tiny.

A man who has an orgasm begins to lose his erection soon after he ejaculates. This is a response built right into our bodies. For some time after a man has an orgasm, he cannot get another erection. For young men, this period when erection is impossible can be as short as a few minutes, but this period lengthens to a few hours for mature men and then to many hours or even a day or two for elderly men. There are drugs that men can take to get erections faster and easier; you see these advertised on TV all the time. These are legitimate drugs because there are medical conditions, such as diabetes, that interfere with nerve functioning and blood flow in the genitals and make it harder for men with those conditions to get erections. However, often these drugs are overused or misused.

## How Can a Dream Be Wet?

Many boys experience their first ejaculation in their sleep. Doctors call this a nocturnal (or "night") emission, but most people just call it a wet dream. Wet dreams seem to occur naturally and are nothing to worry about or feel bad about. We already discussed how it's normal for boys to have erections three or four times every night, usually during a dream. Sometimes during a dream, men will get sexually excited and have an orgasm with an ejaculation. Sometimes this seems to happen with dreams that are about sex. A young man may wake up after having a wet dream and realize he was dreaming about sexual intercourse, about kissing a girlfriend, or simply about talking with a girl that he really likes. Often, however, young men have wet dreams and can't remember their dreams having anything to do with sex. This, too, is perfectly normal and nothing to feel guilty about. We cannot control what we dream.

Wet dreams are normal. You may have to change your underwear or wipe the semen off your sheets, but there is nothing abnormal or bad about having wet dreams. Many boys, though, never experience wet dreams, and this is perfectly normal too.

## SUPER TRANSFORMER

You are being transformed into an adult. Many changes have occurred in your body, and many more changes lie ahead in how you feel, how you will respond to women, and what is going to happen with your life. All of these changes are gifts from God. God wants you to use His gifts very carefully and bring Him glory. He wants you to have the best life possible.

# CHAPTER FIVE

# HOW DOES A WOMAN
# BECOME
## PREGNANT AND
## GIVE BIRTH?

B ecoming a parent can be one of the most wonderful events in your life. It is a miracle how a baby is conceived, develops inside the body of its mother, and emerges into this world as a tiny, new person.

But pregnancy and childbirth are not always such wonderful events. When a teenage girl gets pregnant outside of marriage, it changes the course of her whole life. An unmarried woman may suddenly find that the man who whispered, "I love you; I'll always be with you; I want to share my life with you," suddenly drops her when he finds out she is pregnant. Many men not only do not marry the woman they got pregnant but also refuse to contribute any money or effort to care for the child, leading to legal and emotional battles.

How does someone become pregnant? Whether the pregnancy occurs in the right way (in the context of marriage) or in the wrong way (outside of marriage), the biological realities are amazing.

### NOW, THAT'S PLANNING AHEAD!

While a man produces millions of new sperm every day of his life after he goes through puberty, a woman actually has all of her eggs before she is even born! These eggs are preserved without change through her childhood years. Each egg is tiny, smaller than the period at the end of this sentence. But this is gigantic compared to the size of sperm produced by the man's body.

The sperm and the ova are somewhat like seeds but are different in one important way. An apple seed, for example, has everything necessary in it to grow an apple tree except for nutrients from the outside. But neither a human sperm nor an ovum has everything in itself to grow another human being. In fact, the most critical elements for growing a human being are the chromosomes that contain our genes, and the

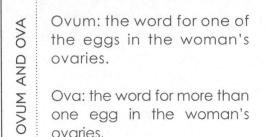

**OVUM AND OVA**

Ovum: the word for one of the eggs in the woman's ovaries.

Ova: the word for more than one egg in the woman's ovaries.

sperm and the egg each have exactly half of the chromosomes that are needed to create a new human being. The chromosomes of the sperm have to join with the chromosomes of the egg to start a new human person.

This is why every human being is physically unique—one of a kind. Human beings are formed from the chromosomes of a mother and the chromosomes of a father. These unique chromosomes combine to make a new pattern that has never been seen in the human race before. There has never been anyone exactly like you, and there will never again be anyone exactly like you.

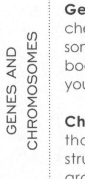

**GENES AND CHROMOSOMES**

**Genes:** tiny strands of chemicals that control some aspect of your body, like what color your eyes will be.

**Chromosomes:** thousands of genes strung together in a group.

A man's body is always producing sperm; his body is always ready to help create a new baby. But a woman's body is only ready to create a baby at certain times. As a woman is finishing a menstrual period, her body is beginning to get ready for the possibility of pregnancy. Her hormones cause her ovaries to produce a single mature ovum (or egg) and to prepare it to be released. Several ova (or eggs) go through the process of maturing, but usually only one is released and able to be fertilized by joining with a sperm.

About ten to twelve days after a woman has stopped her menstrual flow, her ovary releases the mature egg, which is drawn into a fallopian tube. At the end of these tubes are fingerlike struc-

The ovum and the sperm each contain half the chromosomes needed to make a whole and complete human being.

tures that wave gently over the ovary inside the woman's abdomen, creating a movement that draws the egg into the tube. The egg travels down the fallopian tube. The trip is only a few inches, but it takes several days. The mature egg that is released by an ovary can be fertilized by a sperm for only about twenty-four hours. If a sperm does not meet and penetrate the egg during that time period, the

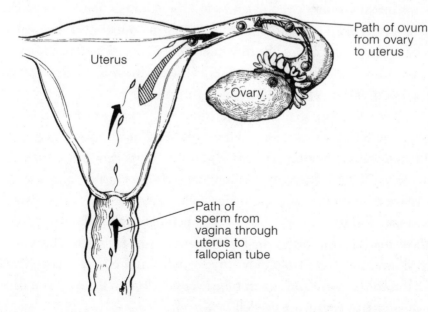

Path of ovum from ovary to uterus

Uterus

Ovary

Path of sperm from vagina through uterus to fallopian tube

egg degenerates (dies) and passes out of the woman's body with her menstrual flow at the end of that cycle. She will not become pregnant during this month.

Some women can tell that they are ovulating because they feel a wetness in their vagina. This wetness comes from their cervix (it's not the same as vaginal lubrication). Some women actually can feel a slight twinge inside their abdomen when an ovary releases an egg. But most women don't know for sure each month when they can get pregnant. Certain women ovulate very early in their cycle, whereas others ovulate late.

**OVULATION** the time when a woman's ovary releases a mature egg that can then join with a sperm.

There is really no time of the month when a person can be guaranteed that ovulation has not occurred and pregnancy is impossible.

## How Does Pregnancy Happen?

When a man and a woman have sexual intercourse, the man's penis goes inside the woman's vagina and soon the man ejaculates. When he ejaculates, between 150 and 600 million sperm come out of his penis into her vagina. Sperm are like tiny microscopic fish, with a head and a tail that whips about to make them very efficient swimmers. Soon after they are out of the penis, they begin swimming.

Because sperm are so tiny, their journey from the woman's vagina up through the cervix, the uterus, and most of the fallopian tube, where one of them may join with the ovum or egg, is very long! Few sperm make it all the way. Of the average 200 million that start the journey, only a fraction make it out of the vagina and into the uterus. And only a fraction of those make it through the uterus to the openings of the fallopian tubes. Of those that make it this far, half go into the wrong fallopian tube. Only a small amount—probably only fifty to two hundred—of those that make it into the correct fallopian tube ever get close to the egg. You can see why so many sperm are needed.

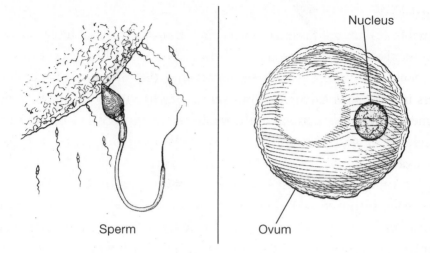

Nucleus

Sperm | Ovum

But it takes only one sperm to **fertilize** an egg. The instant that sperm penetrates the outer layer of the egg, it becomes impossible for any other sperm to get inside the egg. Doctors say that the egg has been fertilized when the one sperm has gone into the egg. This is actually a complex and mysterious event. Scientists used to speak of the "sperm penetrating the egg," but now we know that the egg actually cannot be penetrated until it releases a special hormone that allows it to be penetrated and that the egg participates in drawing in the sperm. Once the sperm is inside the egg, the sperm's head comes apart, releasing all of its chromosomes, the genetic material of the man, into the inside of the egg. These chromosomes from the man quickly join with the chromosomes of the woman. At this moment, a baby has been conceived.

Sexual intercourse is not the only way that pregnancy can happen. Any action that puts sperm in the woman's vagina or on her vulva can cause her to get pregnant because the sperm might swim into her vaginal lubrication as they do what they were made to do: seek out an egg. Also, you may have heard how some couples who are having trouble getting pregnant will use **artificial insemination**. With artificial insemination, a woman gets pregnant not by having sexual intercourse but by having the sperm of her husband placed inside her vagina or uterus through a plastic tube inserted by a doctor.

## IS GETTING PREGNANT HARD OR EASY?

Women do not get pregnant every time they have sexual intercourse. As we said earlier, the egg can be fertilized for only about twenty-four hours before it begins to break apart and die. Sperm typically live between one and three days, but some may live up to five days. This usually means there are about three to five days each month when a woman can get pregnant. If she has sexual intercourse two or three days before she ovulates, her husband's sperm may be up in the fallopian tubes and still alive right when the egg is released. This egg might get fertilized early in its journey down the fallopian tubes. On the other hand, if the husband and wife have sexual intercourse just as the egg is released, the egg may stay alive just long enough for the fastest sperm to reach it. Sometimes, for reasons we don't understand, the sperm simply fail to reach the ovum. And sometimes, even though they reach the ovum, fertilization does not take place; either the sperm can't penetrate the egg or they just miss it.

It may seem that it is hard to get pregnant. Many things can go wrong. Some couples who really want a baby find they have trouble getting pregnant. But it is much easier for most young women to get pregnant than many of us realize. Just under one million teenage women get pregnant every year, and most of them did not mean to. Most women do not know with certainty when they ovulate, and we don't ever know exactly how long the man's sperm might live. Some people try to prevent pregnancy by guessing when the woman is going to ovulate, but those guesses are often wrong.

People also try to prevent pregnancy in ways that are quite ridiculous. For instance, an old story says that if a woman gets up immediately after having sex and jumps up and down, she will shake most of the sperm out of her vagina and will not get pregnant. This method does not work. Sperm begin swimming immediately when they get inside the vagina, and even if most of the semen shakes out by jumping up and down, enough sperm stay inside the vagina to easily get the woman pregnant. Some couples also think that if they stop having sexual intercourse before the man has an ejaculation, there is no way the woman can get pregnant. This, too, is wrong because there is often a tiny drop of fluid that comes from a man's penis even before he ejaculates, and this tiny drop sometimes contains live sperm. It takes only one sperm to get a woman pregnant.

## How Do Twins Happen?

Any birth of more than one baby is called a multiple birth. Multiple births include twins (two babies), triplets (three), quadruplets (four), and so forth. There are two types of multiple births. One happens when only one egg is released and gets fertilized. The other occurs when the woman releases more than one egg and more than one get fertilized.

**Identical twins** start off the same way all single births do, with the woman releasing one egg, which is fertilized by one sperm. But something happens very early, possibly even before the developing baby attaches to the inside wall of the uterus. For unknown reasons the fertilized egg, which begins to divide into smaller and more cells, does something

> **MULTIPLE BIRTHS**
> when a woman gives birth to more than one child from a single pregnancy.

that usually doesn't happen. It splits completely in two and begins to develop as two babies rather than one. These two babies started from the same single cell and so have the exact same chromosomes. Because it's the chromosomes that cause us to have certain physical characteristics, these twins will look just alike. Remember earlier when we said that every human being is different? Well, the one exception to this is identical twins, who are genetically exactly the same. They do become unique and different, however, because they are distinct persons in God's eyes and also have unique and different experiences.

If the woman releases two (or even three or four) eggs, and if each joins with a different sperm, the woman will have twins (or triplets or quadruplets) that are not identical; they are called **fraternal twins**. Because each fraternal twin comes from a different egg and different sperm, they usually look no more alike than do other brothers and sisters in the family.

They have no reason to look identical, as their chromosomes are just as different as a brother's and sister's born five years apart.

Nothing can be done to cause a woman to have identical twins, and no one is sure why it happens. Fraternal pregnancies appear to happen because some women's bodies just release more than one egg on a regular basis. Also, some drugs that doctors give women who are having trouble getting pregnant cause the women's ovaries to release multiple eggs, so women on these drugs are more likely to have multiple births than other women. Births of four babies or more rarely happen without use of these drugs.

## How Does a Woman Know She's Pregnant?

One of the first signs a woman has that she is pregnant is that she doesn't have her next menstrual period when she expects it. The purpose of the menstrual cycle is for the woman's uterus to get ready to become pregnant. Once she is pregnant, there is no need to get rid of the blood and tissue inside of the uterus. In fact, the developing baby needs the extra blood from the mother to give it oxygen and food. While women are pregnant, they normally don't have any bleeding or menstrual flow.

Just because a woman misses her period doesn't mean she is pregnant. Sometimes women don't have their menstrual flow at the normal time because they have been sick, very upset, or tired, or for some other reason.

About two weeks after a woman has missed her period, some unique chemicals appear in her urine and blood that, when tested, will definitely show whether or not she is pregnant. About the same time, if a woman is pregnant, she begins to experience some other signs, such as mild nausea. Because most women have this sick-to-their-stomach feeling more frequently in the morning, it's called morning sickness. This nausea can last from several weeks to several months.

## The Rest of the Story

After the egg is fertilized, it continues down the fallopian tube for about a week until it comes into the uterus. At first it is only one cell with a mixture of chromosomes from the woman and the man. But even as it journeys down the fallopian tube, it begins to divide. One cell splits into two, two into four, and on and on, slowly at first. But the dividing soon picks up speed, and this begins the remarkable growth of the baby. Within a day or two, it has become a compact ball of cells that is the same size as the original egg.

The next critical stage is for this tight ball of cells that is the developing baby to attach or stick to the side of the uterus. This is called **implantation**. If the tiny ball of cells that forms the baby implants, it is likely to grow and be born a healthy, whole baby. If it doesn't implant but continues down the uterus and through the cervix, it will die from lack of nutrition and simply be passed out of the body. Usually when this happens, the woman never knows that her egg was fertilized and a new life was conceived. No one knows why some babies implant and others don't.

If the baby implants, it continues to develop rapidly. With nourishment that it receives from the uterine wall, it now begins to grow and divide. At first the dividing cells all look the same, but very quickly different cells form different organs and begin to perform specific jobs. At the time of this early growth, some of the cells form a **placenta** right where the baby connects to the wall of the uterus. The placenta is an organ with lots of blood vessels in it that takes oxygen and food from the blood of the mother in the wall of her uterus and absorbs them into the blood of the baby. From the placenta, the **umbilical cord** carries these nutrients into the baby's body. The umbilical cord connects to the baby's body at its navel, or belly button. Other organs that will sustain the baby begin to form right away. A tiny brain begins to form, followed by a tiny spinal cord. The internal organs start to form: heart, lungs, and liver. Arm buds, leg buds, and a tail begin to form. The tail disappears later, while the arms and legs lengthen and the baby's other parts grow and develop rapidly.

The rapid development of the baby is incredible. If we grew as fast after we were born as we did while we were in our mother's uterus, we would be the size of elephants by the time we reached four or five years old. We grow from one cell tinier than a grain of sand to an average of seven or eight pounds and about twenty-one inches long within the span of nine months. Now, *that* is astounding growth!

For reasons not well understood, some babies die after they begin to grow in the mother's uterus. This is called a **miscarriage**. Research suggests that babies who die before they are born often have something seriously wrong with their bodies, something that would make it impossible for them to live. But no one knows why most miscarriages occur.

### IS THERE ENOUGH ROOM?

How does a pregnant woman's body make room for a baby? Her uterus, normally the size of her closed fist, grows large enough to hold even a ten- or eleven-pound baby. So to make room for this baby, her belly stretches outward, but also her other internal organs get pressed and pushed out of the way. For example, toward the end of their pregnancies, most women find they have to go to the bathroom much more often because their bladders are pressed and not able to hold as much urine as they used to. Also, many pregnant women end up eating several small meals instead of three regular meals during the day because their stomachs and intestines are so compressed that they can't hold as much food as they used to.

> Your navel is the scar that was left when your umbilical cord dried up and fell off after you were born.

Pregnant women often experience muscle aches, as their bodies are not used to carrying the extra weight that comes with pregnancy. Women commonly gain a total of twenty to thirty-five extra pounds during pregnancy. That weight gain includes the weight of a seven-to nine-pound baby, plus weight gained because of other changes in their bodies. One change that always occurs is in their breasts. Women's breasts usually grow in size as the milk ducts expand and get ready for milk production. That milk production is called **lactation**.

## It Sounds like a Lot of Work

Nobody knows what begins the process of labor, but after about nine months, the woman begins to experience labor pains. This is because the uterus, which is made of sheets of muscle, is squeezing and forcing the baby down lower. The strongest muscles in the uterus are at the top, and they begin to contract to push the baby out through the cervix and vagina.

For the average woman, labor lasts about fourteen hours for the first child and shorter for other children. During those hours, the cervix, which is normally closed, is slowly forced open. God made women's bodies so that their hips are able to stretch and flex so the baby can go through the circle of bone at the base of the hips and on through the cervix and out the vagina. If the entire birth process takes fourteen hours, the first thirteen are required just to get the hips and cervix to open large enough for the baby's head to come through. Once they are open enough, the birth proceeds very rapidly.

The woman begins to push hard to get the baby through the cervix and through the vagina. The vagina, which is normally quite a small tube, stretches during the birth process to let the baby come through. The normal way of delivery is for the baby to come out headfirst. As the woman pushes, the baby's head, which is specially designed to force the cervix open and pass through the vagina, appears in the outside world for the first time. As the woman continues to push, the rest of the baby's body comes out. The doctor cuts the umbilical cord after the whole baby is out to disconnect the baby from the placenta. Within minutes after the baby comes out of the woman's vagina, the rest of the umbilical cord and placenta comes out as well.

> **LABOR**
> the hard work of giving birth to a baby.

Childbirth hurts. Don't let anyone tell you otherwise. But a woman's body is very resilient, designed by God just for this purpose. After giving birth to a child, a woman is extremely tired and overwhelmed with how much pain and work it was, but she is also overjoyed with

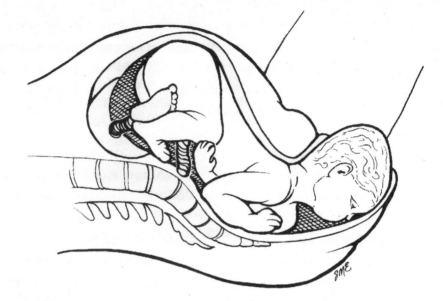

the fabulous, miraculous gift of her baby. She is able to hold it and be with it right away.

It takes a number of months for a woman's body to return to normal. The uterus, which was so stretched out of shape, slowly returns to normal. The woman usually loses much of the extra weight she gained. Her hips return to their firm condition, and her vagina and cervix heal from the stretching they went through.

Not all babies can be born through the vagina. Sometimes when babies are not in the head-down position but are bottom down and head up, doctors decide it is too big a risk to give birth to the baby through the vagina and so deliver it through an operation. Doctors also sometimes deliver babies through operations when a woman's passageway through her hips is not big enough to let a big baby be born or because they are afraid that a baby may not be strong enough to survive the difficult process of being pushed through the vagina. This operation is called a Caesarean section. Doctors give the mother an anesthetic that makes her numb to pain, and then they make a cut right above the woman's pubic hair through the muscle to the woman's uterus. They carefully cut through the wall of the uterus and remove the baby through this incision. Then they sew the wall of the uterus, the muscles of the abdomen, and the skin back together. The woman has a healthy baby even though the baby was not delivered through the vagina.

## GETTING THE RIGHT START

Just as God made women's bodies to care for babies before birth, He made women's breasts to feed their babies after they are born. During the first few days after a baby's birth, its mother's breasts give out a substance called **colostrum**. Colostrum has some food value, but this watery, yellow liquid mainly acts as medicine for the baby, helping it resist diseases and infections that might threaten its life in its first few weeks out in the world.

Within several days, the mother's milk begins to be produced; this is called lactation. The milk that is made in a human mother's breasts is the perfect food for babies. Babies would be malnourished and grow up abnormal if they were fed nothing but cow's milk. When a woman is lactating, she eats more than she normally would because her body uses up extra food making the milk. The milk builds up in her breasts over two to three hours. Then when the baby begins to suckle on her breast, milk is released from the milk glands to flow out of her nipples. For many different reasons, some women choose to feed their babies specially designed baby formula rather than nurse them with their own breast milk.

Most babies live on nothing but their mother's milk (or formula from a bottle) for five to eight months before mothers begin to give them other kinds of simple foods they can digest. Some babies will stop nursing soon after they begin to eat solid foods, while others continue to nurse, though much less than they used to, for months and even years after they begin to eat solids.

What a miracle that any of us are born! What a gift God gave us in our sexuality and ability to have children. What does God say about how we should handle this beautiful gift? That's our next subject.

# CHAPTER SIX

# WHY SAVE
# SEX
# FOR MARRIAGE?

Sometimes it seems everyone is having sex. Some kids in high school talk as if they have sex all the time. Not many kids admit to being a virgin, the word for anybody who has not had sexual intercourse yet. In many groups, "virgin" is used as an insult instead of a virtue. Characters on television and movies often move quickly from their first meeting to a bedroom scene. In many school sex-education classes, there is much more talk about using birth control when you do have sex than about choosing not to have sex. A teenager who chooses not to have sex can feel a little lonely!

People will try to convince you that saving sexual intercourse for marriage is stupid. They will tell you things like:

- "Sex is the very best way to express affection and love. If you really love someone, you will have sex with him or her."
- "You must have sex to be a mature, normal, and grown-up person."
- "You simply must have sex. The desire for sex is so strong, it cannot be resisted."
- "It's important to try sex before you get married to make sure you are sexually compatible."
- "It is important to have sex to practice for marriage."
- "Sex is always good."

It's important that you know that every single one of these arguments is terribly wrong. But . . .

### If They're Wrong, What's Right?

One of the most important things for you to do is decide what you believe about sex. Beyond just the facts about our bodies, which we have talked about in the last four chapters, what do you believe sex is for and how should it be used?

Christians believe that God intentionally made the sexual parts of our bodies to be wonderfully sensitive. He gave us the capacity for great pleasure. Of course, non-Christians also believe that our bodies are good and able to give us great pleasure, but one way in which we Christians are different from people who don't believe in God is that we believe our bodies are *gifts* from God.

We treat gifts differently than we treat things we have made or bought. If you work to earn money and then use that money to buy a game or piece of clothing, you may feel you can do anything you want with it, maybe even give it away, break it, or destroy it. But we usually don't feel that way about gifts. We see a gift as an expression of love and caring from another person. And it's right to feel that way about the gift of sex. It's important to think about how God wants us to use that gift.

We adults feel a special longing in our hearts for someone special to love and be loved by for our entire lives. God made sexual intercourse to be a special "glue" that helps hold two people together for a lifetime of marriage. The Bible teaches that when two people have sex, they become "one flesh." The first time it teaches this is in the story of how God made the very first human beings: "That is why a man leaves his father and mother and is united to his wife, and they become one flesh" (Genesis 2:24).

What does it mean for two different people to become one flesh? Nobody fully understands this mystery. God does not give us the answer in the Bible. But even though it's a mystery, it's true: Sex was meant to keep on bonding two people together for life. When a husband and wife have sexual intercourse, they completely share their bodies with each other. If they genuinely love each other and can share their lives with each other, then having sexual intercourse can truly be what people call it: "making love." The couple will have sex because they love each other, and they will love each other more because they have sex. They share their whole bodies because they share their whole selves. The Bible teaches us just how special this gift of sexual intercourse is and why it's worth waiting for; we will discuss this further below.

> Sexually transmitted diseases, or STDs, are spread by people having sex. Their germs are either concentrated in a man's semen or a woman's vaginal lubrication or are most easily spread through the delicate tissues of the man and woman's genitals.

There are three great reasons to save sexual intercourse until you are married: to be safe, to honor God by obeying Him, and to honor the very purpose and meaning of sex.

## Reason 1: To Be Safe

You've probably heard people talk about the importance of "safe sex." That's because sex can be very dangerous. There are two big physical dangers of sex outside of marriage. The first is the risk of sexually transmitted diseases (STDs), such as chlamydia, HPV (human pappilomavirus), trichomoniasis, genital herpes, gonorrhea, syphilis, viral hepatitis, genital warts, and others.

One of these STDs, syphilis, can kill you when left untreated, but all have serious consequences. It is important to realize just how serious some of these diseases are, so let's look closer at the three most common STDs:

**Chlamydia** is a bacterial infection spread by sex. If detected early, it can be effectively treated. But sadly, chlamydia has no noticeable symptoms, so infected people rarely think they have a disease and never get diagnosed and treated. But don't think it is harmless just because infected people don't notice they have it! The chlamydia infection can spread through a woman's body and produce scar tissue in a woman's uterus and fallopian tubes. If untreated, it can leave the infected woman unable to ever have children.

**HPV (human pappilomavirus)** is a viral infection estimated to be the most common and rapidly spreading STD. At this time, there are no known cures for HPV. Like chlamydia, it usually has no noticeable symptoms (except those varieties that cause warts on your genitals and elsewhere). People with HPV are often completely unaware of it. Women who get HPV are at great risk for developing cancer of the cervix (which is the point where the vagina joins to the uterus) later in life. This is a very serious and dangerous cancer.

**Trichomoniasis** is an infection from a type of protozoa, a single-celled parasite that flourishes in the urinary tract of a man and the vagina and urinary tract of a woman. Men rarely have any symptoms of infection, and some women have no symptoms. People who have trichomoniasis are more vulnerable to being infected with HIV, and women who have it are more likely to deliver premature babies if they get pregnant.

We didn't yet mention the most deadly STD: HIV (Human Immunodeficiency Virus), the infection that results in AIDS (Acquired Immune Deficiency Syndrome). HIV is a virus similar to that which causes the common cold but is a much more deadly type of virus. HIV gets into the cells of a person's body and begins to kill the specialized cells made in the body by the immune system to fight diseases. If untreated, an HIV-infected person rapidly becomes less and less capable of fighting off other diseases and eventually dies from one of these other diseases. It is this state of having a weak immune system and having many other

> STDs are more common today than at any other time in history. Several studies have shown that over one-third of all college women have already had at least one STD by the time they are twenty-one years old!

infections that is called AIDS. People don't really die of HIV; they die from other diseases that their body could have protected them against had HIV not wrecked their ability to fight off that disease.

HIV/AIDS is a terrible disease. Early on, almost everyone who got HIV died of AIDS within a few years. Now we have drugs that help people with HIV (who are called HIV-positive) live much longer; some people have lived twenty years or more with the disease and may live a normal life span. They are never cured of HIV and will get sick if they stop

> **HIV:** human immunodeficiency virus
> **AIDS:** acquired immune deficiency syndrome
>
> HIV AND AIDS

taking their medicine, but with treatment they can live fairly normal lives. Unfortunately, they can still infect other people with HIV for as long as they live. In 2006, we know that about twenty-five million people have died of AIDS since the disease first appeared in Africa, and about forty million people have HIV, most of them in Africa but more than one million of them in the United States.

HIV is mostly spread by sexual contact. HIV spreads throughout the infected person's body but is especially concentrated in the blood, semen, vaginal lubrication, and breast milk. Almost all the people who have HIV got it from having sex with someone who had it. But not everyone gets HIV this way. Some people get it when they take drugs from a needle that has HIV on it. Some children were infected by their HIV-positive mothers who, without meaning to, passed it to their babies through their own blood during pregnancy or after birth through their breast milk. A few others got infected through blood transfusions before doctors knew how to make sure blood was clean from HIV.

All sexually transmitted diseases can be passed by a person with the germs in his or her body to the person he or she has sex with. It's been said that when you have sex with someone, you are having sex with every other person your partner ever had sex with. What does this mean? Let's say you know a sixteen-year-old girl who has never had sex before, and she chooses to have sex with her eighteen-year-old boyfriend because she feels "in love." Is she safe because she has never had sex before? Suppose her boyfriend has had sex with three other women before your friend, and one of those other women had sex with six different men. If one of those six men had HIV, chlamydia or HPV, he may have passed it on to that girl, who in turn passed it to her new boyfriend, who is now likely to pass that disease to your friend. This is the way sexually transmitted diseases are passed.

You are probably asking, *How can I be sure I never get one of these sexually transmitted diseases?* The answer is simple. If you save sexual intercourse and all sexual intimacy (we talk about what this means in the chapter on dating) for the person you marry, and that person also saves sex for marriage with you, then neither of you ever has to worry about having a sexually transmitted disease.

There's a second physical danger of sexual intercourse. It's almost always possible for the woman

> About one million teenage women get pregnant each year. About half of those, approximately five hundred thousand young women under twenty, choose to have their babies aborted.

to get pregnant when a couple has sexual intercourse. Many medical problems result from a woman getting pregnant when she is a teenager. Babies born to teenage mothers are more likely to be born underweight or premature. A teenage mother is more likely to be hospitalized or have other medical problems as a result of her pregnancy.

The physical risks aren't the only concern. The basic options for a young woman who is pregnant are to abort the baby, have the baby and give it up for adoption, or keep and raise the baby. A young woman who chooses to have an abortion will have to go through life knowing she let a doctor kill the baby inside her body because she didn't want that baby. Giving a baby up for adoption is a wonderful gift to the adoptive parents and to the baby who will be raised by parents who deeply want the baby and are ready for parenthood. But going through the pregnancy changes the young woman's life, and giving the baby up for adoption is a hard experience.

If she chooses to have and keep the baby, the young woman's friendships may change when friends pull away from her because they don't want to share that experience with her and can't relate to what she is going through. Teenage mothers are more likely to drop out of school and to live in poverty because they can't get a job. Teenage fathers are less likely to help with the baby or help support the mother with money than are married, mature fathers. There is lots of research that shows that children who grow up with only one parent are not as happy as children who grow up in families with two parents. The children do not do as well in school, get into trouble with the police more, and are more likely to have children of their own while they are still teenagers than are children whose parents are married and both active in raising their children. All of the options are hard ones when a young, unmarried woman gets pregnant.

## What About Condoms?

Many people will say that while sex outside of marriage is never completely safe, it can at least be made "safer" by using a condom. There are condom advertisements on television, posters, and everywhere today. What are condoms?

A condom is shaped like a balloon, and most are made of a substance called latex, the same material doctors' gloves are made from. The condom rolls over a man's penis and is supposed to be left on the whole time the couple has sexual intercourse. The condom does two things when it works right. First, it catches the man's semen when he ejaculates. Because the semen does not go into the woman's body, she shouldn't get pregnant. Second, the condom prevents the skin of the man's penis and his semen from touching the inside of the woman's body and her vagina, and that helps prevent germs from crossing from his body to hers, or from her body to his.

Condoms do make sex physically safer; there is no disputing this fact. People who use condoms are significantly less likely to get pregnant or catch an STD than people who have sex without using a condom. But how safe do condoms make sex? Imagine you have a seven-year-old brother and you live near a big highway. One day when you are baby-sitting your brother, he says he wants to play on the highway. You know that letting him play on the highway would be deadly. Would you let him play there? Of course not. But suppose he asks that you let him play on the shoulder of the road, where the cars don't usually drive. Is that a good idea? Suppose he asks to play on the hill right next to the highway where he could accidentally roll down the hill onto the shoulder of the road. Would this be all right because it's safer than playing on the highway itself?

> Jesus answered, "I am the way and the truth and the life. No one comes to the Father except through me. . . . If you love me, keep my commands. . . . Anyone who loves me will obey my teaching. My Father will love them, and we will come to them and make our home with them. Anyone who does not love me will not obey my teaching. These words you hear are not my own; they belong to the Father who sent me."
>
> (John 14:6,15,23-24)

When people have sex outside of marriage, sex is physically safer if they use a condom than if they don't. But they are still taking risks. People who use condoms don't get pregnant nearly as often, but they do get pregnant. They do not get diseases nearly as often, but they do get diseases, including HIV. Medical professionals who strongly recommend condoms still admit that they are less than perfect. They estimate how well they work by estimating how often a couple who had sex regularly for one year would wind up with the woman pregnant. If that couple did not have sex at all, the chance of pregnancy obviously would be 0 percent. If they do not use a condom or any other method of birth control, the chance of pregnancy would be 85 percent. And if they use condoms regularly, the chance of pregnancy is estimated to be 15 percent, and this assumes that both people are mature and experienced at using condoms. That's better than 85 percent, but there's still a significant chance of pregnancy.

Why aren't condoms completely effective? Well, sometimes they break. Sometimes they have tiny holes that can't be seen but are big enough for germs and semen to get through. Also, condoms often fail to work because many people, especially teenagers, don't use them correctly. Condoms fail more often with teenagers than with adults. And while condoms are effective in stopping those diseases spread exclusively through the semen and vaginal fluids, there are some sexually transmitted diseases that condoms do not stop. The worst example is probably HPV. HPV spreads over the skin, and so while using a condom will stop HPV transmission through the skin of the penis, it will not stop *other* skin contact that can transmit HPV (like the man's scrotum touching the woman's labia during sex).

> Flee from sexual immorality. All other sins a person commits are outside the body, but whoever sins sexually, sins against their own body. Do you not know that your bodies are temples of the Holy Spirit, who is in you, whom you have received from God? You are not your own; you were bought at a price. Therefore honor God with your bodies.
>
> (1 Corinthians 6:18-20)

The physical consequences of sex outside of marriage, specifically pregnancy or disease, are truly scary. One reason to save sex for marriage is to stop these bad things from happening to you. But this is not the most important reason to wait to have sex until you are married.

## REASON 2: TO SHOW GOD YOU LOVE HIM BY OBEYING HIM

A second and vital reason for not having sex outside of marriage is because God does not want you to. Jesus once said, "If you love me, you will obey what I command." God wants us to show our love for Him by the way we live our lives. We can honor God with our hearts and minds by believing and trusting in Him. And we can honor God with our bodies by using them to do good and by not doing the things God doesn't approve of. The Bible teaches that when we save sexual intercourse for marriage, we are honoring God with our bodies. Obeying is a way of showing who we love. We can show God who we really love by what we do with our bodies.

The physical dangers of sex we talked about in Reason 1 are only part of the story. Sex before marriage also puts you in spiritual danger. Why? Because the Bible teaches that obeying God helps us grow close to Him, and disobeying God often causes us to drift away from Him. Young people who misuse the gift of their sexuality by having sex before they are married are not only taking physical risks but also gambling with their relationship with God. They are gambling that they can disobey God and still stay in a loving relationship with Him.

> We know that we have come to know him if we keep his commands. Whoever says, "I know him," but does not do what he commands is a liar, and the truth is not in that person. But if anyone obeys his word, love for God is truly made complete in them. This is how we know we are in him: Whoever claims to live in him must live as Jesus did.
>
> (1 John 2:3-6)

## Reason 3: To Honor the Very Purpose and Meaning of Sex

God made sex to be a special bond between a husband and wife in marriage. Remember that Genesis 2:24 verse? "That is why a man leaves his father and mother and is united to his wife, and they become one flesh." Sexual intercourse unites two people. It bonds them, glues them together, joins them in some mysterious way that the Bible itself does not explain. Sex is a life-uniting act. It was meant to be used as a special gift in marriage, a way to help bond two people together for life. If we use it any other way, such as to have fun or prove that we are a real man or woman, we are doing the wrong thing with this gift. Have you ever glued something together and realized later you made a mistake? You might get it apart, but the residue of the glue is always there. Or you might break it in the process of taking it apart. Misusing God's gift of sex glues you to the wrong person, and you'll probably get hurt.

Sex outside of marriage can hurt us not only physically and spiritually but also emotionally. Because sexual intimacy unites two people, sexual intercourse with the wrong person can do emotional damage to us. Mike feels that because he had sex before marriage it is harder for him to really feel bonded to his wife. Kristin feels like a piece of her heart was broken to pieces by having sex with her boyfriend, who later broke up with her. Maybe sex before marriage is one reason why so many people now find it hard to have good marriages later. Many more people have sex before marriage now than used to be the case. As the number of people who have had sex before marriage has gone up, so has the rate of divorce. By having sex with people other than our husbands or wives, we may be breaking down our ability to really unite with the person we marry. It is like bonding together with another person and then ripping apart again over and over. If the person who has had sex is really sorry and asks God to forgive and heal him or her of this damage, we believe God can and will help that person. But shouldn't we protect ourselves from this kind of damage in the first place by not having sex outside of marriage?

> Do you not know that your bodies are members of Christ himself? Shall I then take the members of Christ and unite them with a prostitute? Never! Do you not know that he who unites himself with a prostitute is one with her in body? For it is said, "The two will become one flesh."
>
> (1 Corinthians 6:15-16)

> Scientific studies show that people who have had less sex before marriage are happier with their marriages, enjoy sex more in their marriages, and divorce less often than people who had more sex before they were married.

Being united, one flesh, with your husband or wife is a complicated thing. We (Stan and Brenna) had sexual intercourse for our first time on the night we were married. It is true to say that we became one flesh that day, after exchanging our vows, celebrating our marriage, and making love for the first time that night. But there is a sense in which being one flesh is something we are still working on thirty years later and will always be working on. Sex is a vitally important part, but only part, of becoming one.

So it is important to understand what sexual intercourse does not do: Sex is meant to unite two people, and it does unite or bond them, as the Bible teaches. But this doesn't mean that any two people who have sex are married or must stay together. A person who's had sex with two or ten or more people is not married to all of those people. And people who have sex as teenagers should not feel they must marry their sexual partners. Marriages that start out this way often end in divorce and disaster. People who have had sex before marriage should commit themselves to not having sex ever again before they marry. They should pray that God would forgive them for breaking His rules and release them from the effects of joining themselves to someone they were not married to.

Look deep in your heart. Which sounds like the better life to you? Would you like to stay single all your life, perhaps having sex with five or ten or fifty people? Or would you rather have one person whom you truly love, whom you marry and stay bonded to for life, having and raising children together until death parts you? If the second type of life sounds better, then saving sex for marriage is a good idea.

THE LIES YOU WILL HEAR

But many people will try to convince you otherwise. They will say:

1. *"Sex is the very best way to express affection and love."* We've all heard it: "If you really love someone, you will have sex with that person." The truth is that sexual intercourse *is* one of the best ways of expressing true love, the love that goes along with the lifelong commitment of a marriage. And the best way to find out whether the love you feel is the kind of real love that will last a lifetime is to *not* have sex before marriage.

Instead, take the time to really get to know and love the person you are feeling so good about. You don't have to have sex to express love. You can express your love for each other through kindness and thoughtfulness and by just enjoying all the good and wonderful things about being with the person you love.

2. *"You must have sex to be a mature, normal, and grown-up person."* Some people will hint that if you haven't had sex, you must still be a kid. But who is really the mature person? The person who goes along with the crowd and believes what the television and movies tell her to believe, or the person who believes God and the Bible and has the strength to do what is right even when many people around him aren't? The Bible says a mature person has self-control, knows that loving and obeying God is what is really important, and is wise and strong. And a mature person doesn't need to have sex before marriage.

3. *"You simply must have sex."* Here's the lie you will hear: the desire for sex is so strong that it cannot be resisted. But Jesus lived for thirty-three years on the earth and never had sex. Millions of Christians have lived their whole lives single and never had sex, while others have saved sex for marriage over many years. Today over half of the girls who graduate from high school have had sex at least once. But just thirty years ago, less than twenty girls in every one hundred had sex by the time they graduated from high school. If we have to have sex, how could people at other times have chosen not to have sex? Even today, young women in Japan and many other cultures have sex before they marry much less frequently than do young women in America. It is a lie that we must have sex.

4. *"It's important to try sex before you get married to make sure you are sexually compatible."* This statement means that you should try sex with different people until you find someone with whom sex is very good; then you can be more confident in marrying that person. This is terrible advice. What makes two people sexually compatible, what makes their sexual relationship full of joy and pleasure and beauty, is

the quality of the love they share and their desire to please each other. There is no special, magic way two bodies fit together that makes sex great; you do not have to "shop around" and have sex with twenty people to find the "best fit." A loving married couple *creates* sexual compatibility by learning how to please each other better and better the longer they live together. Two people who truly love each other will work to improve their sexual relationship over the years of their marriage so their joy with each other can grow more and more.

5. *"You need to have sex now to practice for marriage."* The idea here is that the more you have sex before marriage, the better you will be at it and the better sex will be in your marriage. But as we just said, the couple who saves sex can have the joy of practicing and learning to love each other better after they are married. Also, scientific studies show that people who have sex with lots of people before marriage have *less* happy marriages, more divorces, and less happiness with sex in marriage. There is actual scientific evidence that people who live by God's rules are more likely to have better marriages and better sex lives.

6. *"Sex is always good."* Do television shows and movies focus on someone getting pregnant or catching a disease after casually having sex? No. Was sex good for the thousands of people who now have sexually transmitted diseases, including HIV and AIDS? Was sex good for the almost one million teenage girls every year who get pregnant? Was it good for the over half-million babies born to teenage girls who aren't married, or the over 250,000 that are aborted by their mothers? Was it good for the girls who had sex because their boyfriends lied and claimed to love them and a month later moved on to another girl? Sexual intercourse is not always good.

## WHY SOME PEOPLE CHOOSE SEX BEFORE MARRIAGE

Given these reasons, why would anyone choose sex before marriage?

Some teens believe some or all of the arguments we just discussed. But there are many other reasons people choose to have sex before marriage.

Some people have sex for the pleasure of it. Is this a good reason? No. First, while sex can actually be pleasurable, it is not nearly as pleasurable for many teenagers as the movies and television programs suggest. For many women, especially, it takes the love and concern and sharing of marriage to make sex its best. Many young women who have sex as teenagers have a neutral or unpleasant experience with sex because it happens without the love and care that marriage provides. Second, many teenagers seek the pleasure of sex because they have no purpose for their lives other than to have as much fun as possible. Their lives lack the important purposes of loving, serving, and worshiping God. Some guys may think, *Why shouldn't I have sex if that is the best way to have a good time?* For them, having sex is a way to try to fill up an empty space in their lives. But only the love of Christ can fill up your life. God made sex to be a pleasure that a man and woman can gradually grow to enjoy in their marriage, not something to play around with on a date with a person you hardly know.

Some teenagers have sex because they are lonely. Girls who don't have deep friendships with their girlfriends often wind up having sex with boys. We all need friendships. Girls who don't have good friendships will often give sex to boys in order to make the boys more interested in them. It's as though they are buying friendship with guys by having sex. Lonely guys also long for sex to help them feel close to someone. Having sex makes you feel close for a few minutes, but it doesn't satisfy you the way real love can. The lonely person needs the real love of some good friendships and the kind of real romantic love that waits until after marriage to have sex. Most important, the lonely person needs to find out how the love of God can fill his or her heart. Sex is not the medicine to heal the lonely person's hurts.

Some young women think that having a baby who depends on them and belongs to only them will make their loneliness go away. This almost always results in disaster. That baby will love its mother. But it will also change the girl's life forever, pulling her further away from friends and making it even harder to meet a man who can be her husband. The mother often winds up even more lonely. Some guys also try to "make a baby," not because they want someone to love but because they think you're a real man when you get a girl pregnant. This, too, usually results in disaster.

Some kids have sex because they give in to pressure. The teenage years are a time when it's very painful not to be liked by all of your "friends." If you are a teenage girl with a group of girlfriends who are having sex, you'll probably get teased and pressured to lose your virginity. Guys can be pretty ruthless with each other. Some guys will accuse a boy who does not have sex of being homosexual or crazy or of secretly being a woman. Having sex because of pressure doesn't make anyone like you or love you more. It only proves that you don't have the strength to stand on your own to do what is right.

A special kind of pressure can come from the person you are dating. When your parents or grandparents were dating, it was almost always the man who would try to put pressure on the woman to have sex, and it was generally expected that the woman would always say no unless she was a "dirty" sort of woman or a prostitute (someone who has sex for money). Now pressure to have sex is almost as likely to come from the girl as from the boy. Either one may ask, beg, or demand to have sex, saying things like, "I just want us to be closer in our love" or "If we don't have sex, I'm going to explode" or "You say you love me, but the real proof of love is making love." Some people aren't strong enough to stand up to this pressure, so they choose to have sex.

Some people have sex because they are very insecure—they don't have a firm idea of what they believe or what kind of person they are, so they can't feel good about who they are. They try to find ways to feel better about themselves, like having other people tell them that they are liked or have "passed the test." People may challenge you to prove your manhood (or womanhood) by having sex. Insecure people may do what others challenge them to do so those other people will say they're "cool" or okay. It is a terrible idea to have sex to get approval. Having sex proves nothing about you except, perhaps, that you are foolish and weak.

People have sex for many other reasons. Many guys want sex because it is a "conquest." It makes them feel superior to get what they want from a girl, and some guys will do anything to get that conquest. It is wrong to use another person to make yourself feel superior, especially when the way you are using that person — sex — is meant to be an act of love and unselfish giving. This, like all of the other reasons we have given for having sex outside of marriage, is not a good reason. The only good and perfect reason to have sex is to express joy and pleasure and union in marriage.

### Summing It Up

Billboards, magazine covers, television shows, movies, and even "friends" will all tell you lies about sex and what will make your life good. By saving sexual intercourse for marriage, you will be pleasing God by your obedience; you will be protecting yourself against physical diseases, pregnancy, and emotional pain; and you will be preparing yourself to build a marriage of real unity and love. You probably feel you're too young to think about these things, much less to make such big decisions about your life, but you are not! Now is the right time to think and pray about these matters and to decide which way your life will go.

# CHAPTER SEVEN

# LOVE AND DATING

The last time you saw a boy and girl on a date holding hands, gazing into each other's eyes, or perhaps hugging and kissing, how did you feel about it? Did it seem disgusting, or was it appealing?

Before they go through puberty, most kids think love and dating are gross. But by the time they are fifteen or sixteen years old, love and dating sound wonderful (and maybe a little frightening). By that age, many kids have felt they were "in love" a number of times.

Part of how we feel about love and dating is wrapped up with how we feel about other people's bodies. Before we go through puberty, most of us have a child's curiosity about other people's bodies. But after puberty, our interest in our bodies is more than just curiosity; it can include powerful feelings of excitement and desire that are strange and unsettling. Our feelings about sexual intercourse and other ways of being physically close, like kissing, change too. What seemed gross when we were nine or ten no longer seems that way.

## What Makes Me Change My Mind?

Part of it is probably due to actual changes in the way your brain works. The same hormones that cause your body to mature also change your brain and the way your mind and feelings work.

Your thinking about sex is also a result of your maturing as a person. Part of being a child is being dependent on your parents and longing to have them protect and take care of you. Part of being an adult, on the other hand, is being independent and starting a family of your own. To do that, you need to have a love relationship with one special person from outside your family. So feeling sexual desire and love is part of the normal process of maturing and becoming independent of your family. God wants you to grow up and feel those things because it is part of His plan for you as an adult.

So what does it mean to date, and who should you date? Let's talk about dating and some of the problems and challenges it presents.

### It's a Date!

Here's a scene: A guy pulls into a girl's driveway in the car he's borrowed from his parents. Maybe he honks the horn, or maybe he goes up and rings the doorbell. The girl comes out and they go out for the evening—to a play at school, a football game, dinner and a movie, or maybe bowling. They enjoy their time together, and the boy brings her home approximately thirty seconds before the absolute deadline her parents gave her for being home. That's what many people consider a "date" or "going out."

But dating isn't always that way. In our community, some kids start "going out" in the seventh or eighth grade. The funny thing to us parents is that kids who "go out" often don't actually go anywhere. "Going out" means that a boy and girl like each other and talk to each other on the phone or exchange notes or talk at school.

Dating is really just an opportunity to get to know another person you particularly like. One of the best ways to get to know another person when you are fourteen or fifteen is to have that person join your group of friends in a church or school group activity. Having that person come to your youth group, join your Bible study, or go with your friends to the mall can be an opportunity to find out what kind of person he or she is without a lot of pressure or expectations.

As you grow older and start to have more definite interests in a certain person, it is usually possible to spend more time with him or her at activities such as those just mentioned. You can discuss with your parents the possibility of meeting this person at a school basketball game or a church event.

As you get older yet and desire to spend even more time with this one particular person, it can be fun to "group-date" with two or three couples, going on something like a hike or bike ride, going to the movies, or doing a service project for your church.

Finally, you can begin to have dates when you spend special time just with this person you like. We suggest that young people not do independent dating until they are at least sixteen years old. By independent dating, we mean the kind of dating where a young man and woman

> Do not be yoked together with unbelievers. For what do righteousness and wickedness have in common? Or what fellowship can light have with darkness?
>
> (2 Corinthians 6:14)

are on their own to do the activities that they choose (with the permission of their parents). By waiting until you are sixteen, you will have more confidence in your ability to take care of yourself since you will be old enough to drive and get a job. You also will have had some experience in handling yourself in challenging situations, so if something is not right, you can take care of yourself.

## Does It Matter Who I Date?

The Bible instructs us that it is not wise for a Christian to marry someone who is not a Christian. Why? Most married people discover just how important it is that both partners in the marriage look at life the same way. It adds strength to your marriage if you both believe in God, can pray together, value the same things in life, believe the same things are right and wrong, and can enjoy your involvement in serving and worshiping God together in your church. Couples who don't have a common bond of faith often find that their different views of God slowly become more painful and difficult.

We believe that it is very important for Christians to date only other Christians. Be careful about continuing to date a person who does not share your faith; you may help that person's faith grow stronger, but he or she may make your faith grow weaker. And the weaker your faith, the poorer the choices you might make. If the other person is a Christian, you have a good basis on which to get to know him or her further.

## He Loves Me, He Loves Me Not

One of the most frightening, wonderful, confusing, and joyous experiences of the teenage years is falling in love.

These feelings come in so many different varieties they are hard to describe. When you are just beginning to be interested in the opposite sex, you may find yourself thinking that a certain person is especially nice. You feel as if you want to do things for that person, and you want that person to be a special friend. When these feelings grow stronger, you can get pretty swept away by them. Some teenagers find themselves thinking about a special person all the time.

Especially in the early teenage years, some kids love to tease and taunt others who are obviously having romantic feelings toward another person. Someone may pick on you with embarrassing questions or crude comments if they learn that you are "in love" with someone.

Sometimes grown-ups are not much better. They can be insensitive about what you feel are real love feelings. A parent might call those feelings "puppy love" or some other name that implies they aren't real. Sometimes a parent will even say, "Oh, you aren't really in love." This kind of reaction by adults is understandable because, believe it or not, your parents and all of the adults around you have had the same feelings. Most parents who see their child going through the process of being "head over heels in love" remember all the times they had similar feelings at your age and how those relationships almost always fell apart in disappointment. This can make parents a little skeptical about your feelings.

Do you want to find out something new about your parents? Talk to them about the times they were in love when they were teenagers. Ask them to tell you how they felt and what kind of things they did as a result of feeling like they were in love. Get them to tell you about the times they "went steady," about the silliest thing they did to express their affection, about what it felt like to be in love, and also what it felt like when a relationship broke up.

While a skeptical adult reaction is understandable, it is also unfortunate. It treats the real feelings of a teenager as if they are unimportant and mistaken. A teenager's feelings should be treated with respect and care. What you feel are real feelings, and they are precious and beautiful. God made you capable of feeling strong caring and affection, and that is a very special gift from God.

### TAKE THE TEST

But even if those feelings are real and a gift from God, that doesn't mean the love you feel when you are thirteen or sixteen or nineteen is a mature love. There are only two tests that will show whether love is mature or not. The first is the test of time. We remember times from our teenage years when we felt passionately, wildly, almost crazily in love with another person, and it was amazing how two weeks later we no longer had those feelings. A love that is true will stand the test of time as you get to know the other person better and better. True love finds out more of who the other person really is and grows to appreciate more and more about that person.

The second test of mature love is the test of restraint. A love that is true will grow slowly over time as the couple acts toward each other in the way God wants them to. Having too much of a physical relationship can actually prevent you from getting to know each other better.

There is one other thing young people should know and understand about feelings of love. They are almost always connected with the sexual feelings of our bodies. God made us so that the more feelings of love and infatuation we have, the more sexual feelings and desire we feel.

When you're a young child, your feelings of love toward your family go naturally with a desire to hug and kiss and touch them. This is a way you express your love with your body. The attraction and love feelings you have as a teenager include this desire to hug or kiss, but the romantic feelings are different and stronger. You may have noticed that couples who seem really "in love" touch each other a lot, holding hands and putting their arms around each other. Some moms and dads act this way toward each other; they hug and kiss their children, but the hugs and kisses and pats they give each other are different from those they give their children.

God made us so that our feelings of love or attraction are connected to having sexual feelings about the person we love. When a fourteen-year-old boy thinks about the girl he has a crush on, he may find himself with an erection—a sign of sexual excitement. A fourteen-year-old girl may notice a slight wetness in her vagina when she thinks about a boy she is attracted to. These feelings do not mean that this boy or girl is thinking about sexual intercourse or even about the other person's body; it only means that God made us so that our feelings of love and interest in another person are connected with how our bodies respond sexually. This is a great gift because later, when you are fully an adult and married, your sexual relationship with your wife or husband will be a wonderful way for you to express your love. After you go through puberty, you will begin to respond to feelings of love as a whole person (body, mind, emotions, and spirit), like an adult. This is something to celebrate and not to be embarrassed about or feel guilty about.

As a teenager, you may find yourself thinking how wonderful the person you are in love with looks. You may like hugging and holding the other person or thinking of being married to him or her. All of these feelings, and even the feeling that having sexual intercourse with the person would be wonderful, are part of the natural way we respond when we have feelings of love. God makes us capable of these kinds of feelings, but it is vital that we use this gift the way God intends. Many teenagers today wrongly believe that if you have any feeling that something sexual would be fun or exciting, you should go ahead and do it.

Just because we have feelings of wanting something does not mean that it is right for us to have it. It is a good gift from God when a teenage couple in love are excited by each other and interested in each other, but God does not want them to choose to have sex. Sexual intercourse is to be reserved for marriage. By choosing not to have sex, a couple can take the time to really get to know each other and have a clear sense of whether this is the person God wants them to marry. Having sex with a person you are not married to hurts you and hurts the relationship you will someday have with your husband or wife. It also hurts God because having sex outside of marriage is disobedient to God's command and a signal to Him that we do not love Him with our whole heart.

## To Touch or Not to Touch

Okay, we know that having sexual intercourse is something we are not supposed to do before marriage. Are there ways people can express affection or be sexual in dating that are okay in God's eyes?

This is a difficult question, partly because it's embarrassing to talk about. But it's also hard because the Bible doesn't talk directly about these things. Is that because God doesn't care what we do as long as we don't have sexual intercourse? We believe the answer to that question is no.

The Bible does not talk directly about this subject because "dating" as we know it did not exist in the times the Bible was written. Most people lived in very small towns and villages. Even the large cities of ancient Palestine were small by today's standards. Marriages were arranged, which means that parents would make the decision about who their children would marry. It was not uncommon for children to grow up knowing who they were going to marry. People would often marry young, almost always before they were twenty. Couples would not often be left alone because it was important that they not have sex before they were married. They had none of the privacy young couples have today where they can hop in a car and drive twenty or thirty miles away from anyone who knows them. In that ancient culture, God didn't need to speak of rules for how people should behave when they dated, because they didn't date. Often they got to know each other only after they were married.

But the Bible does give us good principles to guide us in our moral choices. To apply that advice to the situation of dating today, we have to be clear about what can happen sexually in dating. Human beings have been very creative in what they do for sexual excitement and to make their bodies feel good sexually. Even a simple touch on the shoulder or pat on the back can feel exciting if the person who touches you is someone you like or love. A couple might hold hands or put their arms around each other. It's very common for couples to kiss when they have feelings of love for each other. But there are kisses, and then there are *kisses*. A kiss may be a very simple peck on the cheek or the lips. Or, instead of a quick peck, the couple may kiss with their lips for a little bit longer. And then there is passionate kissing that you have probably seen on television or in a movie when the couple seems stuck together for minutes. This kind of kissing is called French, or deep, kissing. The man and woman open their lips and touch their tongues together as well as their lips. (We don't know of a single young child who, when he or she first hears of this, doesn't say, "That is the most disgusting thing I've ever heard; I will never do that!") Our advice is to save your kisses for a very special person.

In spite of what the movies and television programs show, most couples do not go directly from passionate kissing to having sexual intercourse. Some couples who are very attracted to each other gradually share more and more of their bodies with each other without having sexual intercourse. When a person feels strong feelings of love for another, it is natural to want to touch the other person's body, even his or her private parts — the woman's breasts and both partners' genitals. When teenagers let the other person touch their private parts or when they touch the other person's private parts, they are doing something that is much more intimate than just kissing. The intimacy gets even greater if the couple begins to unbutton or take off their clothes so they are sharing even more of their bodies. Instead of touching the other person through their clothes, they may directly touch the other person's uncovered breasts or genitals. These and the many other ways in which people touch each other without having sexual intercourse are called petting. This is an awkward name. We usually think of petting pets, not people. As you listen to other kids talk, you may hear other slang words that mean the same thing as petting.

Such touching can be more or less intimate. A young man may briefly touch a young woman's crotch while she is wearing jeans, and this is intimate, but less intimate than if she lets him pull her pants down and fully touch her genitals. Some couples touch each other's genitals—the girl rubbing the boy's penis and the boy touching her vagina and clitoris—to the point of one or both of them having an orgasm. This is very intimate, yet they have not had sexual intercourse. One of the most intimate things a couple can do short of having actual intercourse is called oral sex ("oral" for "with the mouth"). A girl performs oral sex on a boy when she takes his penis in her mouth and rubs it with her tongue and lips until he has an orgasm. A boy can perform oral sex on a girl by using his tongue and lips to caress her vagina and clitoris. In some teenage circles today, oral sex is becoming more common and not regarded as "having sex."

Let's call all of this "sexual intimacy." You can see how the intimacy gets deeper and deeper, more and more personal, and how both people are sharing more and more of their bodies, as they go from kissing to petting to oral sex.

What does God think of such sexual intimacy? As we said already, the Bible doesn't give any direct rules about sexual intimacy, but in Matthew 5:27-30, Jesus talks with great seriousness about the problem of adultery. He emphasizes that the Bible speaks against people having sex with someone they are not married to and then goes on to say, "I tell you that anyone who looks at a woman lustfully has already committed adultery with her in his heart" (verse 28). Jesus seems to mean that what we do with our thoughts is just as important as what we do with our bodies. We should do more than just keep our bodies from doing things that break God's rules; we should also try not to have desires or thoughts about breaking God's rules. These words of Jesus suggest that it is very unwise for teenage couples to engage in sexual intimacy. When a couple becomes more sexually intimate, they are encouraging their hearts and minds to think about sex more and more. This can lead them into exactly the kind of lustful thoughts Jesus was speaking against.

Also, the reason the Bible tells us not to have sexual intercourse with someone we are not married to is to protect us against being bonded or glued to someone we are not married to. Sexual intercourse provides that special kind of bonding. But people who engage in extensive sexual intimacy often experience some of this kind of bonding because they are sharing much of their bodies openly with another person. In sexual intercourse you share all of your body with the other person. But in petting you begin the process of sharing your body, and when you engage in intimate petting and oral sex, there is very little left of your body that you have not shared.

Speaking of protection, we must mention also that if teenagers engage in full sexual intimacy, particularly direct touching of the genitals or oral sex, they are at risk of getting the same sexually transmitted diseases that are transmitted through sexual intercourse. Anytime the body's sexual fluids — semen or vaginal lubrication — come in contact with another person, such transmission can occur. With more teenagers engaging in oral sex, sexually transmitted diseases of the mouth are becoming more common.

Lastly, sexual intimacy can be dangerous simply because people who do it often get very sexually excited, and when they are excited they do not make good decisions. A teenager may feel confident that she should not have intercourse. But if she starts some petting with her boyfriend, she may find herself thinking, *This is so exciting that I bet I can handle a bit more . . . and a bit more than that . . .* Many teens who wind up having sexual intercourse were not planning to do so before they got going in petting.

The reason we wanted to tell you about these things is so that you can think about them and make a decision about what you will and will not do before you even start developing a close relationship with another person. We urge you to decide now that you will be careful with the precious gift of your sexual body. By choosing not to have sexual intercourse with anyone before you marry and by choosing to keep your body private and special by not petting, you are honoring God. You are making the gift of your body that much more special for the person that you may marry someday. If you stay single, you are protecting yourself from possible problems and are giving the gift of your body to God, just as He wants (see Romans 12:1-2).

## SOME REALLY GOOD ADVICE ABOUT DATING

- Keep your other friendships going while dating; don't depend on dating as your only kind of friendship.
- Don't start dating too early. You have plenty of time to learn about love, so take your time.
- Ease gradually into dating as you are ready and as your parents agree you are ready.
- Relax. Enjoy a friendship rather than pursuing your possible spouse.
- Date only Christians. Your companions will affect who you are.
- Be accountable to your parents for definite plans for dates. Do what you say you will do.
- When on a date, avoid movies and TV shows that focus on sex or that aim to get viewers sexually excited.
- Dress modestly for a date. Don't send out mixed signals.
- Be prepared to talk openly with the person you are dating about your moral standards regarding sex.
- Include prayer in dating, perhaps before and after a date.
- Involve the person you date in the important parts of your life, such as family gatherings and church activities.

# CHAPTER EIGHT

# TOUGH ANSWERS
# TO SOME
## TOUGH PROBLEMS

What if my date tries to force me to have sex? What if my best friend is having sex with her boyfriend? Couldn't living together before marriage prepare a couple for the real thing? What do I do if my sex-education teacher gives advice I don't agree with? Is masturbation evil? My friend thinks he might be "gay" — now what do I do? How can I believe in marriage when my parents couldn't make it work?

As a young person trying to live a life that is pleasing to God, you will face some tough issues. We wish you would not have to face any of the issues we will discuss in this chapter, but maybe our words will help you make good decisions before you do face them or be a better friend to someone dealing with these problems.

## NEGATIVE ATTITUDES TOWARD WOMEN

Scientists and educators who observe how girls develop into women have noticed a very disturbing pattern. In the elementary school years, girls do just as well as boys in school. They feel just as good about themselves and speak up and express their opinions just as freely as boys do. But in the middle school years, many girls lose their confidence. Some stop thinking of themselves as capable and become full of doubt and insecurity.

Nobody quite knows why this happens to so many young women. It may be that some teachers begin to direct most of their attention to the boys in a class, and the girls may be treated as if they were not there. Also, middle school boys begin to respond with excitement and appreciation to girls, but often only to the girls who they think are attractive and who don't act smart and confident. Girls who don't look exactly like fashion models begin to feel left out, and girls who ought to take pride in their musical skills, athletic abilities, intelligence, and capabilities in schoolwork often feel they don't matter.

There are many good things happening for women today, especially in America. Women are able to get more education than ever before. It's becoming more and more common for women to become scientists, doctors, political leaders, lawyers, and businesspeople.

But women continue to be physically abused in their marriages —beaten up by their husbands. Women are treated as sex objects in the media, as having value for only their bodies. The message seems to be, "If you look right, you matter. If not, forget it." In many advertisements, we see a message communicated that women matter only if they look sexy and have numerous men panting over them.

What can we do about all of this? All of us need to think about women and men the way God does. The first truth we have in the Bible about men and women is that they were created equally in the image of God:

> So God created mankind in his own image,
>     in the image of God he created them;
>     male and female he created them. (Genesis 1:27)

The apostle Paul picks up this same idea in Galatians 3:28, where he says, "There is neither Jew nor Gentile, neither slave nor free, nor is there male and female, for you are all one in Christ Jesus."

Women cannot be worth less than men or treated as objects because they are created in the image of God. And we need to act on that belief. Girls need to act in confidence that they are just as loved by and special to God as are boys. Boys who are reading this chapter should remember to treat girls with respect. In the words of Jesus, boys should "do to others what you would have them do to you" (Matthew 7:12).

## THE CHALLENGE OF PRESSURE FROM YOUR FRIENDS

When Blake was in seventh grade, he hung out with a rough group of guys in his neighborhood. One day these friends shoplifted candy from a convenience store and then teased and harassed Blake because he didn't steal anything. Blake knew it wasn't right, but he caved in to their pressure. The next time they went to that store, he also stole and then did so again several times over the next few weeks. Finally he realized he did not want to grow up being a thief. It was painful to choose to stop hanging around with that group of friends and put up with their name-calling and pressure.

Part of being a teenager is wanting to fit in with your friends. In the teen years you are becoming your own person, separate and different from your family even though you will always be part of your family. Having close friends during these years keeps you from feeling so glued to your family and gives you a sense of being a different and unique person. You are no longer just a child in your family; you are now your own person. But how do you make sure you really are your own person and not just someone who does whatever your peer group tells you to do?

Teenagers are often pressured to use cigarettes, alcohol, and drugs. People who do these things are more likely to experiment with sex. They are also more likely to do poorly in school or even be in trouble with the police. Steve gets teased at school for being a virgin. Cindy gets pressure on a date to have sex. How will you handle it when people put pressure on you to have sex or use alcohol? How do you stand up for the truth when it hurts for others to make fun of you?

First, we are always weakest when we stand alone. All of us feel stronger when we know others who agree with us. Of course, we are not really alone if we are doing what is right, because Jesus stands with us. With God on our side, we are a match for anything. "If God is for us, who can be against us?" (Romans 8:31). But even when Christ is for us, it helps to have another person beside us. That's the reason it's so important to be part of a youth group at your church or a Christian group that prays together or studies the Bible at school. You will be more able to stand up to the pressure of other kids when you know you have friends who believe as you do.

> I have set before you life and death, blessings and curses. Now choose life, so that you and your children may live and that you may love the LORD your God, listen to his voice, and hold fast to him.
>
> (Deuteronomy 30:19-20)

Second, handling pressure successfully starts with deciding what you will and will not do. Decide now whether or not you will have sex before you are married. Decide also what level of sexual intimacy you will allow when dating while you are a teenager. Don't wait until you are out on a date or at someone's house to decide.

Think through what we have said in this book. Talk with God about your decision. If you believe that we have been telling you the truth about sex, make these decisions right now. After you make a decision, tell God, your parents, and a Christian friend about that decision. It pleases God when His people make and keep promises to Him.

Third, think through how you will handle pressure. Most of this pressure will come in the form of comments like, "What's the matter with you—are you a prude?" "Haven't you grown up yet, or are you still

> Choose for yourselves this day whom you will serve. . . . But as for me and my household, we will serve the LORD.
>
> (Joshua 24:15)

a child?" "Are you gay or something?" "But we have to have sex or I'm going to go crazy!" "You say that you care for me, but you don't show it by doing what people who love each other do." "If you don't have sex with me, I'm going to ruin your reputa-

tion all over school by telling everyone what a prude you are!" "Please, if we just do it this one time I won't ask again." "You said you'd go out with me, and that meant you'd have sex, so stop being a tease!"

It is not important that you have a snappy, clever answer to any of these comments. It is important that you say no in a way that indicates you really mean it. You do not have to have a long discussion with the person pressuring you. You can simply say, "I do not choose to have sex with you (or kiss you or let you touch me). I want to go home now, and so our date is over." If someone is putting a lot of pressure on you and won't stop, you may have to tell him or her that you'll complain about the person's behavior to your parents, the person's parents, a school counselor, or some authority figure.

Pressure to have sex can sometimes get even worse. A number of girls report being forced to have sex on a date. Sometimes a girl may let herself be talked into having sex, or she may feel threatened by a boy who says he'll ruin her reputation at school. Young women need to be strong to handle these kinds of threats if they occur. No one has the right to force you to do anything you don't want to do. Most people who make threats cannot carry them out, but if they actually do, the things they threatened are not nearly as bad as having sex would have been.

If a person uses threats against you, you should demand to be taken home right then. In extreme cases, you may have to be prepared to fight back physically. God does not want you to be a victim. A slap, a poke in the eye, twisting a finger until it breaks—all of these seem like extreme actions, but they may help you get out of a situation that is out of control and help you preserve your own safety. We know it is scary to talk about these things, but by having a clear idea about what you should and shouldn't do, you can protect yourself and keep yourself safe. And the best thing you can do about this kind of situation is to prevent it from ever happening by knowing well the person you are with, making it clear what your standards are, being sure he is a Christian, and having safe plans for your time together.

## WHEN A FRIEND IS HAVING SEX

One of the hardest things for teens to handle is when a friend reveals to you that he or she is having sex. Robert had counted on Travis as a friend who was committed to saving sex for marriage. Melissa felt that Rachel would always be there to help her stay strong in handling her sexuality God's way. But Robert and Melissa, both seventeen, found that their respective friends had begun having sex with the people they were dating. Travis told Robert that he and his girlfriend still both believed that sex outside of marriage was wrong but that they somehow found themselves going too far and couldn't seem to stop. Rachel told Melissa that she had changed her mind about staying a virgin. She was sure she was in love with her boyfriend, and it just didn't seem wrong to give her body to him when she loved him so much.

> If someone is caught in a sin, you who live by the Spirit should restore that person gently. But watch yourselves, or you also may be tempted.
>
> (Galatians 6:1)

How would you handle it if one of your friends told you he or she was having sex? Every situation is different, and there is no one answer. You must balance two very difficult truths: Your friend needs your help, but having a friend who is having sex may tempt you to have sex.

Your friend needs your gentleness, your help, to get him or her back on the right path. Maybe you can help her see that her boyfriend has been putting pressure on her. Maybe you can help him resist the temptation to have sex. You can gently remind her that sex outside of marriage is a sin that hurts God and hurts the person and that God's gift of sex is too precious to use wrongly.

> Do not be misled: "Bad company corrupts good character."
>
> (1 Corinthians 15:33)

You also have to keep in mind that by talking with your friend about sex, you are in danger of being tempted. When you talk about sex with your friend, your talk may be helping your friend, or it might be hurting you. Kids who have sex often feel guilty, and one way to make that guilt go away is to convince themselves and their friends that sex outside of marriage is okay. You may think you are helping your friend, but he or she may be trying to get you to change your stance on sex. The Bible is very realistic about this; the apostle Paul advises, "Do not be misled: 'Bad company corrupts good character'" (1 Corinthians 15:33). So try to help, but be honest enough to know that you can help only so much. And pray hard about your friend and for yourself in this situation. When you feel that nothing is changing or that your own beliefs are weakening, that is the time to say, "This friendship is hurting me and my relationship with God. I need to back off and just pray for my friend." And make sure you have friends who are helping you stay strong in what you believe.

## What About Pornography?

Pornography means any video, magazine, movie, book, or picture that shows or discusses people having sex or the private parts of the human body in a way designed to sexually arouse people in an unwholesome way. By far, the most common type of pornography today is Internet pornography, where people find endless streams of movies, videos, pictures, stories, sound recordings, and other means to sexually excite and arouse. Billions and billions of dollars are spent each year trying to expose young people to such pornography through pop-up ads and e-mails. Already such pornography is popping up on cell phones and video iPods.

Looking at pornography can be very appealing to teenagers, especially to teenage boys (since most pornography is about women's bodies). All of us are curious about the human body and about sex. Pornographic pictures are made in such a way as to make the person who looks at them get sexually excited. A person might think, *Well, it's not like I'm having sex with anyone, and this isn't hurting anyone else. I'm finding out about sex, and it seems exciting to me. What could be wrong with this?*

Is there anything really wrong with pornography? Yes. The decisions you make as a teenager will shape the kind of adult you become. The Bible doesn't talk directly about pornography, but it definitely suggests that pornography is not good to look at:

- The Bible suggests that who you are sexually is meant to be private, shared only with the person you marry someday. But in pornography, people are sharing their bodies with thousands of other people. Taking pictures of a sexual relationship and making them available to others violates the privacy of sex. It is wrong to make such materials, and anyone who looks at pornography is supporting others doing wrong in making it.
- The Bible says lust is wrong, and Jesus said lust is committing adultery with another person in your heart. When people look at pornography, often it encourages them to think about having sex with the person in the pictures. By looking at pornography, you are encouraging yourself to lust.
- By looking at pornography, you are filling your mind with false images of what sex is like. Pornography usually presents sex as selfish; immature men think it should be. Women are presented acting as sex slaves to men. Sex is not presented as the beautiful, sharing, giving thing God meant it to be. People who have been hooked on pornography say it is very hard to get the memories of what they have seen out of their minds. If you view pornography, then later, when you are trying to learn to love your new husband or wife, these images can be flashing through your mind, interfering with the experience you're sharing with your spouse.

For all of these reasons, we urge you to protect your mind and heart by staying away from pornography. The teenager who uses pornography is training his mind to move away from what God wants.

## Cybersex

It has become very common for young people today to strike up relationships through Internet chat rooms, instant messaging, blogs, and online networks. Other new ways to do this will probably keep popping up in the years ahead. Some of these relationships turn quickly to the topic of sex, and some young people start saying things in these relationships that they would never say in person.

You have already heard from your parents and in the news that some of the people starting these conversations are not other young people your age but rather adult predators, people hunting for a young person to victimize sexually. These men (and they are almost always men) hunt for girls or boys to take advantage of. Young men and women who have been drawn into relationships with such men have been abducted, raped, and murdered. These men become experts at posing as someone your age when interacting on the computer. They learn the current slang appropriate for your age by listening in on kids conversing in chat rooms. Some even have elaborate, made-up identities with false pictures and video so that they seem fourteen instead of thirty-seven. They also try to break down your relationship with your parents and family. They try to create the sense that they can be trusted but your family cannot—that they understand you and that your family does not really care about you.

A recent survey reported that about one in five U.S. teenagers had been solicited sexually on the Internet in the last year. This is an alarming statistic. Such solicitations include not only offers to meet for sex but also requests for a "date," encouragement to engage in sexual talk and discussions, and requests that you send nude pictures or videos over the Internet.

Internet relationships are very dangerous. Although there are people who have developed healthy and good relationships over the Internet, you need to exercise extreme caution in such relationships, and we would strongly recommend that you not have any such relationship without ensuring your safety. The danger of such relationships is based on the fact that they lack the normal accountability of personal relationships. Think about it: If you tell your parents you are riding your bike to the local McDonald's or Starbucks to meet some friends, your parents might ask, "How do you know these kids?" You might reply, "You remember, they go to my school (or their family goes to our church, or they live two blocks away)." These hints give your parents ideas of how they can search for you if you are missing. This is what we mean by accountability. Predators will not tend to take chances in doing anything bad to a kid if they think there is any chance they can be tracked down. This is why Internet relationships are so dangerous: Everything about the relationship can be made up so that there is practically no chance the person can get caught if you are in a secret relationship with them.

Also, teenagers get drawn into acting in ways online that they would never act in public. On the Internet it can seem like everyone is talking trashy. The chances of anyone knowing it is you talking this way seem small, and it is natural to feel curious about whether you can come across as "hot" or sexy in talking this way. Curiosity is a pull too; it can feel irresistible to find out what happens next if you say just one more outrageous thing. Many kids who talk dirty on the Internet feel as though it isn't really even them—the real them—talking this way.

The danger here is that how we act, even on the Internet, *is* part of who we really are. Acting a certain way on the Internet, or at school or in some new situation, has an impact on us. We change who we are, we move toward who we will be in the future, by the decisions we make today. The person who talks trashy on the Internet today is making herself more likely to talk that way again on the Internet tomorrow, and more likely to fall into that way of thinking and acting in real life. Trash talk on the Internet is like a rehearsal, and what we practice we become more comfortable with and more likely to weave into our total personality. This is why we should all avoid sexual and crude talk, even on the Internet—because our decisions shape who we are becoming. And, of course, we all have to ask if how we are acting is pleasing to the God who loves us and made us. Make no mistake: God is not embarrassed or ashamed of your sexuality. He gave it to you as a gift. But when you make choices that abuse or misuse His gift of sexuality, God does get upset because our bad choices fall so short of the beauty He wants our sexuality to reflect.

## Living Together

Many people today live together, including having sex, before they are married. This is called **cohabitation**. Some people think, *There is so* *much divorce. It makes sense to live together before you get married. It's like a trial marriage. Living together gives you a chance to get to know the other person, to make a better decision about whether you want to get married, and to make sure sex with the other person will be good.*

This view is wrong. Cohabitation is wrong, first because God does not want people to have sex outside of marriage. Sex is to be reserved for marriage, not to experiment with before marriage. Second, scientists have been studying the effects of cohabitation for years, and every scientific study agrees: People who cohabit before they marry have more problems and less happiness with their marriage and sexual relationship (and, in turn, an increased chance of divorce) than those who don't. So if you want a happy marriage, living together before marriage will not help you.

## Public School Sex Education

You can learn many useful things in public school sex-education classes. They can give you good information about the biological aspects of sex, including more information about your body than we have covered in this book. Sex-education classes can also be opportunities to find out what your peers in school think about sex.

But sex-education classes can be very discouraging to Christian teenagers. Some teachers assume that most of the kids in the class will be having sex. They may say once or twice that it's good not to have sex before marriage, but then the majority of the time might be spent in a way that assumes all the kids in the class will be having sex and that what they need to study is how to prevent pregnancy and disease when they do have sex. If you are a Christian teenager seriously committed to living your sexual life God's way, this can be very discouraging. It can leave you feeling as if you are the only one deciding to save sex for marriage.

Also, discussions about reasons for not having sex can be a problem. Some teachers and students do not respect Christian beliefs. In a sex-education class, Justin expressed his belief that God wants sex to be saved for marriage. Instead of this belief being accepted and encouraged, he was attacked for being "bossy" and "judgmental," for saying something that made other people feel guilty. Sometimes when a teenager expresses his or her belief about God's view of sex, a teacher turns that view around and makes it appear that the real reason the teen chooses not to have sex is because of fear of sex or a negative view about sex. Teens sometimes hear something like this: "It sounds like you are really afraid of sex. Maybe your family taught that sex is a bad, dirty, and disgusting thing. But many people don't think it is. Why do you have such negative views of sex?" It can be very upsetting to be put on the spot like this in front of classmates.

Sometimes in discussions about different moral positions, Christian kids are asked to role-play as if they believe the opposite of their own views. Teachers will say this is to help you think through all the options before you make up your mind. But it is risky to even pretend that you believe sex outside marriage is okay. It is good for us to think through what we believe and to compare it to other beliefs. But God doesn't tell us to pretend to have other beliefs. God wants us to remain faithful to Him at all times. You may need to tell a teacher that you don't feel you should have to defend a view you don't believe in.

Because many public school sex-education programs assume that most of the kids in the class will be having sex in the next few years, they focus on teaching kids how to use birth control, especially condoms and birth control pills. We have even heard of teens in eighth or ninth grade being required to go to a store and buy a condom. The reason given for this exercise is that it should help kids get over their embarrassment about using birth control. There are several problems with this focus on birth control. First, the general attitude of the class that "all teenage kids are going to have sex and here is how you can do it safely" is discouraging to Christian teenagers who have decided not to have sex. The second problem is that condoms and birth control pills are not perfectly safe. Condoms make sex somewhat safer physically, but not completely safe, especially not emotionally and spiritually. Birth control pills protect the girl from pregnancy but not from diseases. The kind of safety God wants for you comes from not having sex at all until you are married.

We pray that you will choose to save sex for marriage. But some teens, even those who grow up in Christian families, make wrong choices and have sex outside of marriage. When they do, they hurt themselves and they hurt God. If you choose not to follow God's way but instead have sex outside of marriage, then we urge you to use birth control. We don't urge you to do this because sex outside of marriage is okay. It isn't; it is wrong in God's eyes. We urge you to do this because when you choose to have sex you are taking a tremendous gamble with your life and with other people's lives. You can have a disease passed to you and then pass the disease to another person. You can get pregnant or get your partner pregnant. By using birth control, you are not making what you do less sinful.

## MASTURBATION

You have probably heard **masturbation** joked about, but you may not know what it is. Masturbation refers to a person giving himself or herself sexual pleasure by touching his or her own sexual organs. Boys engage in masturbation more often than girls do, maybe because boys grow up handling their penises when they bathe or urinate and tend to be aware of how good it feels when they touch themselves. Many girls are less aware of the good feelings possible from their clitoris, labia, and vagina because they have less occasion to touch themselves and because of the private location of their genitals.

Most boys have tried masturbation at least a few times by the age of eighteen. Many masturbate to the point of having an orgasm and ejaculation. Some girls try masturbation, and some do it regularly.

Many Christian young people feel horribly guilty about masturbation. In some churches, masturbation is discussed as an evil act that is deeply abnormal. But many people think that masturbation is no big deal because it is done in private, doesn't pass diseases or cause any other physical problems, and doesn't cause pregnancies.

How should we think about this as Christians? The Bible doesn't talk specifically about it. It does seem that if masturbation were a horrible evil in God's eyes, it would be directly talked about in the Bible. But it isn't. So is it okay? While the Bible does not talk about masturbation, the Lord Jesus teaches that what we do with our minds is as important as what we do with our bodies. Jesus condemns lust (see Matthew 5:28). He says committing adultery with our bodies is wrong and that committing adultery in our hearts is wrong also.

Lust is more than noticing that someone is attractive; it is deliberately using our minds to imagine sex that God would say is wrong. For example, a woman imagining sex with her husband would not be lust, since God smiles on her love relationship with him. But imagining having a sexual affair with her next-door neighbor would be lust, since God would not approve of that relationship. Many young people who masturbate don't just touch themselves; they also imagine sexual ideas and pictures, like having sex with a classmate. The command of Jesus to not let lust dominate our lives probably means that it is not a good thing for a young man to let his heart be dominated by thoughts of having sex with women he knows or for a young woman to think in the same way about men she knows.

Masturbation is surely not the full blessing God wants for our sexuality. God made our sexual feelings and our bodies for a very special purpose: to be shared with our life partner in marriage. Maybe one reason so many people have confused feelings about masturbation is that it falls short of what God intended our bodies and sexual feelings to be used for, because it is something a person does alone rather than with a spouse. It can be selfish rather than loving. So even though masturbation may sometimes feel physically good, it will never feel complete.

Also, when we dwell on images of sex, we are training our hearts and imaginations to think about sex in a certain way in the future. If you use images in your mind that turn other people into sex objects when you are a teenager, it will be much harder for you to have a happy, giving, loving marriage relationship later on.

Masturbation is usually not such a big issue that people should be overwhelmed with worry about it. Masturbation can become sinful if a person fills his or her imagination with immoral thoughts. But occasional masturbation that focuses on the pleasure of your body and not on lustful images may not be much of an issue with God. There may be more harm done by people punishing themselves with guilt than by the masturbation itself. We do not think that God wants that.

## SEXUAL ABUSE IN FAMILIES

This is a terribly sad topic to have to bring up. People have twisted and misused in many ways God's marvelous gift of sex, but perhaps none is as sad as sexual abuse inside a family. Sexual abuse inside a family is called **incest**. The most common form of sexual abuse within a family is when an older brother forces a younger sister to do things for his sexual pleasure. Caitlyn grew up in a Christian family, but she was only ten years old when her fourteen-year-old brother began making her have sex with him. But not all sexual abuse involves sexual intercourse. An older brother might make his younger sister touch his genitals, or he may touch her genitals so that he gets pleasure from it.

Sexual abuse also occurs when a father, stepfather, uncle, or cousin forces sexual attention on a child. As we discussed with the older brother, this could be sexual intercourse but could also be touching or other experiences. Though most sexual abuse happens to girls, boys can be sexually abused too, sometimes by a woman in the family and sometimes by a man. Kevin was twelve when his older brother began making him do sexual things with him. All of this is terribly evil.

We pray that this has never happened to you. Kids, especially girls, who experience sexual abuse in their families often feel that they have no one they can turn to, no one who can help them escape this awful situation. If you have a friend who confides in you that he or she is being abused, you should definitely talk to your parents and get advice on how to stop it.

If you have been molested yourself, take immediate steps to protect yourself and make the abuse stop. First, talk to your parents, particularly your mother. Mothers often have a hard time believing such a thing is happening in their family, so you need to be prepared to calmly describe what has happened and to insist that you are not making up what you are saying. If for some reason you can't talk to a parent, then talk to your doctor, your pastor, or a school counselor. These people are required by law to take steps to protect you. The top priority is for you to get protection. God does not want you to be abused.

After the abuse has stopped, it is important to get help for emotional healing. Healing of all the bad feelings and memories can be difficult; it's very important that you have someone you trust to talk with about this. Women who go through sexual abuse sometimes are repulsed by the idea of sex, hate and fear men, and have doubts about God. Sometimes children who have been sexually abused become very focused on sex and mistakenly think they have to act sexual to be loved. Many young women who are abused feel horrible about themselves. They feel angry at their own bodies, and they feel it must be their fault. But abuse is not their fault. If you have been abused and somebody has told you it was your fault, don't believe that person. Your body is not bad, sex is not bad, and all men are not bad. We urge you to talk to someone, to pray to God, and to give yourself time to heal.

## Broken Families

Many Christian kids grow up in homes that have been shattered by divorce, separation, or death. Many of you reading this book may live in a family in which there is only one parent in the home. Many of you may live in blended families created by a second or third marriage. Kids suffer a lot when their family breaks up; they often blame themselves for the breakup. Some kids feel a responsibility to get their mother and father back together. Kids feel lonely for the parent who is not there. Kids in blended families face many problems, such as how to develop positive feelings for this stranger who is now a parent and how to get close to siblings they don't know well.

Living in a broken family can make it hard for a young person to think correctly about sex. Kids often do best when they have a parent of both sexes present to talk to. It is important for girls to be able to understand a man's perspective on sexuality, and it's natural to talk to your father about this. Similarly, boys can benefit from talking to their moms about a woman's perspective. But if these parents aren't available, you can ask the parent you live with who would be a good person for you to talk to.

What if your feelings about marriage have been soured by seeing your parents go through a messy divorce? Some of you may be thinking, *Well, I'm a Christian, and I'll follow God's rules about sex, but I don't ever plan to be married because I know how awful that can be.* Sadly, many marriages are painful. But marriage is still a gift from God, and when a marriage is good, it is a tremendous blessing. Don't give up on marriage, but do realize that every marriage involves struggle and sacrifice. For those of us who have good marriages, the joy and blessing we receive is well worth all the struggle and sacrifice. Look around for Christian marriages that represent the goodness that God intends in marriage. These marriages can be a sign to you of the good that is possible.

If you are in a single-parent family where your parent is tired from working so much that he or she doesn't have much energy left over to talk with you or go to your school activities, this can leave you feeling on your own. Talk with your parent about what might be done. It can help to develop Christian friendships through your church or school that can help you stay strong and make the right decisions. You may even be able to get close to the parents of some of your friends.

## HOMOSEXUALITY

A **homosexual** is a person who feels clear sexual desire for people of the same sex (a man for a man, a woman for a woman) and feels little sexual desire for a person of the opposite sex. The word **gay** is used for men who are homosexuals, and the word **lesbian** is used for women who are homosexuals. Often "gay" is used to refer to all homosexuals (males and females) or even to everyone who is not clearly heterosexual. How should we think about homosexuality? This is a complicated area, but here are a few guidelines.

First, homosexuals are people, and they deserve to be treated as people. People who are not homosexual have caused a lot of suffering for gay men and women. We have made it almost impossible for young people who are trying to figure out their sexual feelings to talk about these kinds of feelings without living in fear of ridicule. Some people make cruel jokes about gays and lesbians and spout off feelings of hatred toward them. No one, especially Christians, should hate homosexual people.

That said, the Bible does condemn homosexual behavior. It calls homosexual behavior "detestable" and immoral (see Leviticus 18:22; 20:13; Romans 1:27; 1 Corinthians 6:9). So how should we feel about homosexual people? We should feel the same way we feel toward people who commit adultery, theft, or any other sin. We should recognize that they are children of God, created in God's image and loved by Him, but that God is saddened by and hates what they do.

We live in a time when gays and lesbians are fighting for their way of life to be completely accepted by the church and all of society as a valid alternative lifestyle. There is a growing push to help young people accept and explore their homosexual feelings, even in the early teen years. Gay and lesbian support groups that aim to "help" a young person discover and accept those feelings within himself or herself are becoming increasingly common, and "Gay Pride" activities and organizations are active in many schools. As a result, in many places it is now more common for Christians to be hated and made fun of for their views than it is for gays and lesbians. Christians who accept the teaching of the Bible that homosexual sex is sinful are put down as hateful, ignorant, bigoted, and intolerant. There is tremendous pressure on Christians today to accept homosexuality.

Part of the push for acceptance is based on the widely accepted notion that homosexuality is biologically caused early in life, even genetically caused at conception. The claims in this area are very exaggerated compared to the actual scientific evidence. In fact, the evidence about genetics is very conclusive that either genetics are not a cause at all or are a minor contributing cause. The most conclusive study proving this was conducted in Australia: If homosexuality is genetically caused then all (or at least a very high proportion) of identical twins—twins who are genetically identical—should have the exact same sexual orientation. But this study located twenty-seven men in Australia who were gay and who had an identical twin, but found that only three of their twin brothers were also gay![1] There is much misunderstanding about what the scientific evidence really says in this area, and about what the Bible says as well. After long study in this area, we conclude that the Bible really does clearly condemn homosexual sex, and nothing that has been found in science undermines this moral view.

But what does this have to do with you? For most young people, this is mainly a question about other people who have same-sex attractions. It is an important moral issue of today, perhaps even *the* most pressing moral issue where Christians are out of step with our culture. But for some young people in our midst, this is a pressing personal issue because you may have felt attraction toward people of the same sex.

The major problem with this is that many of us go through a period when our sexual feelings are confusing, uncertain, and troubling. Many boys feel strong sexual desire and find themselves having an erection without any clear understanding of what has them excited. Many boys and girls have dreams of hugging or kissing someone without a clue as to who the person was, or even if it was a man or a woman. Girls often have such strong feelings of love for their girlfriends that they wonder if those are sexual feelings. As we go through puberty, we have a lot of curiosity about the bodies of the opposite sex but also about the bodies of people of the same sex. For instance, in a locker room a boy might look around to see how other boys are developing. He might wonder if his curiosity about other boys means he is gay. If he is caught looking around, other boys may tease him about that and call him awful names like "fag" (a very harsh and unloving name for a homosexual man).

If our society moves to more and more acceptance of homosexual behavior, this might lead more young people to be confused about

---

1. Stan Jones has written extensively about the moral problem of homosexuality. This Australian study is discussed in Stanton Jones and Mark Yarhouse, *Homosexuality: The Use of Scientific Research in the Church's Moral Debate* (Downers Grove, IL: InterVarsity, 2000). He has also written several works designed for general discussion in the church, including a brief pamphlet published by InterVarsity called *The Gay Debate* and a discussion and rebuttal to a gay-affirming theology called "A Study Guide and Response to Dr. Mel White's 'What the Bible Says—And Doesn't Say—About Homosexuality'" (which is available free at www.wheaton.edu/CACE).

whether the feelings they have are those of a homosexual. You see, homo-sexual feelings are not something that only lifelong homosexuals have; heterosexual people can have them too, though they don't feel them as often or as strongly. Many heterosexuals can remember having confus-ing feelings, including some attraction to the same sex, as teenagers. Our sexuality is a complicated thing, and it was made more complicated when sin became a part of every aspect of our lives, confusing us and making us torn by conflicting and evil desires. There is a common myth today that everyone falls cleanly and perfectly into one of two categories: straight or gay. This is often coupled with the belief that if you have any sexual feelings other than heterosexual feelings, you're gay. Neither of these beliefs is true. Many of us experience mixed, complicated attrac-tion to different people, and we are not defined by any one attraction. A boy may see a scene of sexual violence on TV—say of an attempted rape—and feel some sexual excitement. This does not mean that boy is a rapist. It is just a reminder that we have to work hard to make choices that will help us honor God.

Another problem with the growing acceptance of homosexuality as a lifestyle is that it might lead more young people to experiment with homosexual behavior to see if that is their orientation. "How will you know whether you are gay unless you try it?" someone may ask. We have known people who were involved in homosexual practice while they were teenagers—sometimes with kids their own age, sometimes with slightly older kids, and sometimes with adults. The occurrence of this may well increase as homosexual practice becomes more accepted in our culture. You need to make choices that honor God by accepting His teaching that homosexual behavior is wrong and by committing yourself to not experimenting with homosexual behavior. We need to flee from all forms of sexual immorality, and that includes homosexual behavior.

If you do have occasional homosexual feelings as you go through the teenage years, this is generally nothing to worry about. It is part of the normal range of feelings that go along with growing up. If you find these feelings are very strong and you don't have any feelings of attraction toward people of the opposite sex, then you may want to talk to someone you trust about it. An excellent place to start is to contact Exodus International, a Christian organization that ministers to and supports Christian young people who struggle with unwanted attraction to the same sex. Their website, www.exodus.to, is filled with helpful information and advice.

## WHAT IF MY PARENTS DID NOT HANDLE THEIR SEXUALITY IN THE RIGHT WAY?

The most frequent reason parents give us for being uncomfortable talking with their kids about sex is that they are not proud of how they handled their sexuality before they got married. They might be nervous that their kids might ask, "Mom and Dad, did you have sex or live together before you got married?" Parents worry that giving an honest answer may seem like giving permission to a child to behave just as they did. Yet parents don't want to lie to their children, so many parents avoid the subject of sex in hopes that their own pasts will not come up.

How should you feel about your mom's or dad's past? The truth is, you do not need to repeat the past mistakes of your parents. In fact, you have the opportunity to make better decisions than they did and so experience more of the joy and blessing of God's gift of sexuality than they. As we talk to our children about life, our hope is that they will see our weaknesses but not use those weaknesses as excuses to have the same ones. We hope each one of our children will make better decisions than we have and live a better life than we did. Nothing could make us happier.

If your parents are willing to talk about their pasts, talk with them. We tell parents not to explain to their kids any of the details of their sexual pasts but to talk with their kids about how they feel about it now that they have grown as Christians. Most Christian parents who have broken God's rules about sex are able to tell their kids about the pain, suffering, and difficulty caused by their choices.

# CHAPTER NINE

# WHAT KIND OF
# PERSON
## SHOULD I BECOME?

You stand at the very edge of young adulthood. For many of you, a lot of what we've been talking about seems pretty far in the future. But by the time you are in seventh or eighth grade, some of you will already know of kids who are having sex, catching STDs, getting pregnant, getting an abortion, having a baby, and so on. The future is almost here. As your body goes through the changes we have described in this book, God is preparing you physically to be a mature sexual person. But becoming an adult is more than body changes.

Your parents have had a very strong influence on your life. Part of being a baby is being completely dependent on your parents for everything, being under their control and protection. As you go through elementary school, you slowly begin the process of becoming independent from your parents. You develop more of a mind of your own as you spend time away from them and get a better sense of how other people look at things.

Over the next five to ten years, you will become your own person. Growing up means making bigger and more important decisions, and this can make the process pretty scary. If you don't realize it already, it's time for you to understand a very important truth: You are responsible for the kind of person you become. Your decisions and choices determine what kind of person you are and will be. Your parents and friends will still have an influence on you, but it is your decisions that will shape your life.

## "THE DEVIL MADE ME DO IT!"

Are you ever around people who talk as if they never make any choices? They don't say, "I did it because I thought that was the best thing to do" or "I did it because that is what I believed was right." Instead they say things like, "He made me do it!" or "I had to do it or my friends wouldn't like me anymore." This kind of thinking puts all the responsibility for choices on someone else.

But that doesn't change the truth that you are responsible for the kind of person you become. If you helped another kid cheat on a test because she begged you to, she didn't make you do it. You chose to do it because you wanted her to like you. If you look at a pornographic video on the Internet so the guys will stop making fun of you, they didn't make you do it. You chose to do it because you didn't want them to make fun of you anymore. You need to develop the habit of seeing how you are responsible for the decisions you make. Learn to think, *I choose to do it* rather than *I have to do it*. Why? Because people who understand that they make the choices actually make better decisions.

## SMALL IS BIG

You see, you are the one who is responsible for what kind of person you become. And small choices are just as important as big ones! To grow into a truthful adult, you need to make decisions to tell the truth every day in the small areas that don't seem to matter so much, like whether or not you ate all your lunch, whether or not you got your homework done, or what you did with your friends when you were gone for two hours. Sadly, kids who make bad decision after bad decision in the small areas tend later to make really big bad decisions when the pressure is on.

What seem like small, unimportant decisions make a difference in the area of sex as well. Whether you are a mature sexual person as an adult will depend on the kinds of small and big decisions you make in the next few years of your life. Deciding whether you will repeat or listen to dirty jokes today, or watch that pornographic movie at a friend's house, or experiment with kissing at age twelve—these kinds of decisions are as important as the big decisions you will face later, because they all add together to make you who you are.

If the choices you make are so important, what can you do to help make the best choices? What are some good choices you can make now?

Most important, remember that nothing is more crucial than growing in your faith. Even as a young person, you need to decide whether you believe the truth of the Christian faith. You need to decide now who is going to be your number one commitment in life: yourself or God. And once you've decided to make God number one, having a mature faith is not something that just happens to you. It is something you work at all of your life. Faith is like a race, and the race is won by those who have the diligence and strength to keep going, to keep pressing on.

> I press on to take hold of that for which Christ Jesus took hold of me. Brothers and sisters, I do not consider myself yet to have taken hold of it. But one thing I do: Forgetting what is behind and straining toward what is ahead, I press on toward the goal to win the prize for which God has called me heavenward in Christ Jesus. All of us, then, who are mature should take such a view of things.
>
> (Philippians 3:12-15)

## GROWING WITH GOD

So how do you keep going and grow in your faith?

One thing you can do is to make prayer an important part of your life. Prayer is asking things of God, but it is much more than that. Prayer is setting aside time to meet with God, getting quiet and allowing God to speak to us. It's a time to be honest with God and ask Him to point out what is good about our lives and what needs changing. It's a time to ask God to forgive us for our wrong choices and actions and to thank Him for forgiving us.

It's important to take some time every day by ourselves (maybe in the morning or at night) to talk to God and listen to Him as well. And we can pray short prayers all day about whatever is on our mind, such as, "Lord, please help me to be strong and to forgive that bully who always picks on me in this class."

It's also important to read the Bible. The Bible is God's Word. It is God speaking through human writers to tell us about Himself. Someone once described the Bible as a collection of God's love letters to His children. If you don't have a version of the Bible that is written for someone your age, ask your parents to buy you one. If they can't do this, save up your money and buy a copy yourself. Ask a Christian bookstore worker which type of Bible is best for a kid your age. Read it regularly, and God will speak to you. Start with a book of the Bible like John, Matthew, or Romans, and read a section or chapter each day. Think hard to figure out what it means; pray for God to speak to you.

> This is my prayer: that your love may abound more and more in knowledge and depth of insight, so that you may be able to discern what is best and may be pure and blameless for the day of Christ, filled with the fruit of righteousness that comes through Jesus Christ—to the glory and praise of God.
>
> (Philippians 1:9-11)

It's hard to be a growing Christian all on your own, so it's important that you attend a Bible-believing church where people are excited about their relationship with God. Participate in Bible studies and other activities. Get to know older Christian people who can teach you about growing up strong and true. Get to know a group of other Christian young people, because nothing is more encouraging than having others around who believe the way you do.

Obey what God asks you to do. The Bible says that when we don't obey God, our faith grows weak and dies. When we obey God, we get stronger. This book has been about how to obey God with your sexuality as you enter your teenage years. This is very important. But you need to obey God in all areas of your life, including your attitudes, your relationship with your parents, and how you behave with your friends. Even those who try hard to obey sometimes fail. When you fail, tell God what you have done; God will forgive you and make you stronger because you were honest with Him (see 1 John 1:9).

Finally, learn to pay close attention to the consequences of all your choices. Remember that as you grow into an adult, you need to take responsibility for both what you choose to do and the consequences of what you choose to do.

Welcome to the first stages of adulthood! Being an adult can be great, but how your life turns out rests mostly on your shoulders—on the decisions you make about how you will live your life. Thankfully, God wants to be right there with you to help as you make those decisions, giving you His truth and strength and filling your heart with His love and forgiveness. Sexuality is a wonderful part of God's design for your life, but it is up to you whether this gift will wind up as a blessing or a curse. Our prayer for you is that you will use this gift as God intends and that you will be able to celebrate with joy the blessings that flow from your sexuality.

# ABOUT THE AUTHORS

Stanton L. Jones, PhD, is a professor of psychology at Wheaton College and also serves as the provost (academic vice president). He directed the development of the college's doctoral program in clinical psychology. He is the coauthor of *Modern Psychotherapies: A Comprehensive Christian Appraisal* and *Homosexuality: The Use of Scientific Research in the Church's Moral Debate* and has contributed many articles to professional journals and to such magazines as *Christianity Today*.

Brenna B. Jones is a mother whose goals have focused on the nurture and formation of the character of her children. She served as a leader in a Bible study ministry with women for a number of years and now has an active ministry of discipleship and support for women. She has graduate training in biblical and theological studies.

Stan and Brenna are active in teaching about parenting and marriage in their church. They wrote the original versions of the God's Design for Sex series while their three children—Jennifer, Brandon, and Lindsay—were young; now they enjoy their three kids as adults, along with Brandon's wife, Emily, and son, Canon.

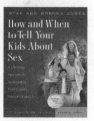